FROM ORDINARY
TO
EXTRAORDINARY

JOHN MACARTHUR

THOMAS NELSON
Since 1798

NASHVILLE   DALLAS   MEXICO CITY   RIO DE JANEIRO   BEIJING

Published in Nashville, Tennessee, by Thomas Nelson. Thomas Nelson is a registered trademark of Thomas Nelson, Inc.

Published in association with the literary agency of Wolgemuth & Associates, Inc.

Thomas Nelson, Inc., titles may be purchased in bulk for educational, business, fund-raising, or sales promotional use. For information, please e-mail SpecialMarkets@ThomasNelson.com.

Unless otherwise noted, Scripture quotations are taken from THE NEW KING JAMES VERSION. © 1982 by Thomas Nelson, Inc. Used by permission. All rights reserved.

Scripture quotations marked NASB, are from NEW AMERICAN STANDARD BIBLE®. © The Lockman Foundation 1960, 1962, 1963, 1968, 1971, 1972, 1973, 1975, 1977. Used by permission.

ISBN 978-1-4002-0269-0 (repackage)

Library of Congress Cataloging-in-Publication Data

MacArthur, John, 1939–
    From ordinary to extraordinary : a year-long devotional to discover what God wants to do with you / by John MacArthur.
    p. cm.
    ISBN 978-1-4002-0241-6
    1. Vocation—Christianity—Biblical teaching. 2. Vocation—Christianity—Meditations. 3. Devotional calendars. I. Title.
BS680.V6M33 2009
242'.2—dc22
                                           2008055787

Printed in the United States of America

09 10 11 12 13 QW 6 5 4 3 2

EXPERIENCE AN
EXTRAORDINARY
RELATIONSHIP
WITH GOD

Have you ever wondered what the people in the Bible were really like, what their relationship with God looked like? Have you wondered if you could know God in the same way?

In the pages that follow, John MacArthur gives you a daily look at some Bible heroes drawn from his bestselling books *Twelve Ordinary Men* and *Twelve Extraordinary Women*. Starting with an overview of how God interacts with his people (the section titled "From Ordinary to Extraordinary") and then continuing with the Bible characters, this devotional gives you a unique opportunity to discover some secrets of their faith.

As you read, the name at the bottom of each page reminds you which character you are studying. Additionally, title pages throughout let you know what characters you will encounter in the weeks ahead.

God longs for your daily walk with Him to go from ordinary to extraordinary. Our prayer is that your day-by-day visit with these exceptional Bible characters will inspire you and show you how.

CONTENTS

JOHN 6:67–68

Then Jesus said to the twelve, "Do you also want to go away?" But Simon Peter answered Him, "Lord, to whom shall we go? You have the words of eternal life."

All but a few would not accept the words of Jesus. Among those who stayed with Christ were the Twelve, whom He had personally selected and appointed to represent Him. They were perfectly ordinary, unexceptional men. But Christ chose to work through the instrumentality of those few fallible individuals rather than advance His agenda through mob force, military might, personal popularity, or a public relations campaign. From a human perspective, the future of the church and the long-term success of the gospel depended on the faithfulness of that handful of disciples. There was no plan B if they failed.

His plan has not changed after two millennia; He still calls perfectly ordinary, unexceptional people to represent Him in the world. If you have received His gift of eternal life, you, too, have been called. What is your answer?

LUKE 17:20–21

Now when He was asked by the Pharisees when the kingdom of God would come, He answered them and said, "The kingdom of God does not come with observation; nor will they say, 'See here!' or 'See there!' For indeed, the kingdom of God is within you."

The strategy Jesus chose to redeem the world typified the character of the kingdom itself. His kingdom is not built upon clever political maneuvering or superior weaponry. "'Not by might nor by power, but by My Spirit,' says the LORD of hosts" (Zechariah 4:6). A dozen men under the power of the Holy Spirit are a more potent force than the teeming masses motivated principally by a selfish desire to be healthy and wealthy.

I encourage people to take stock of their lives periodically and establish goals. As you do, let me challenge you with a few questions. Are you seeking the kingdom of God above all earthly treasures? How are you using your life and your gifts for the advancement of Christ's kingdom? Are you consciously dependent on the Spirit's power for the work of the kingdom?

MATTHEW 16:24–25

Then Jesus said to His disciples, "If anyone desires to come after Me, let him deny himself, and take up his cross, and follow Me. For whoever desires to save his life will lose it, but whoever loses his life for My sake will find it."

J esus chose the Twelve and invested most of His energies in them. His program of preparing them to build and lead His church occurred in four distinct phases, which I believe establish a pattern for our own discipleship:

Conversion – They embraced Him by faith.

Ministry – They exchanged their plans for His.

Apostleship – They became emissaries of His Word to the world.

Martyrdom – They ultimately gave their lives for the sake of the gospel.

Most of us will not be asked to lay down our lives in one dramatic act of sacrifice. Instead, the Lord calls us to surrender them one day at a time. Does that sound severe? Not to worry. The life He offers in exchange far outweighs the one we forfeit.

ACTS 3:12-13

So when Peter saw it, he responded to the people: "Men of Israel, why do you marvel at this? Or why look so intently at us, as though by our own power or godliness we had made this man walk? The God of Abraham, Isaac, and Jacob, the God of our fathers, glorified His Servant Jesus."

I f you've ever visited the great cathedrals in Europe, you might assume that the apostles were larger-than-life stained-glass saints with shining halos. It's a shame they have so often been put on pedestals as magnificent marble figures or portrayed in paintings like Roman gods. That dehumanizes them. It suggests they benefited from some kind of superhuman strength when faced with struggles similar to ours.

They were completely ordinary men—perfectly human in every way. They became extraordinary because they allowed the Spirit of God to have His way within them. They accomplished great things because they worshiped a great God. This makes them heroes we can emulate. After all, believers today are indwelt by the same Spirit of God who empowered them.

JOHN 15:18–19

"If the world hates you, you know that it hated Me before it hated you. If you were of the world, the world would love its own. Yet because you are not of the world, but I chose you out of the world, therefore the world hates you."

I recently read a biography of William Tyndale, who pioneered the translation of the Scriptures into the language of the people. The church leaders of his day, incredibly, did not want the Bible in the language of the people because (like the Pharisees) they feared losing their ecclesiastical power. But against all opposition, Tyndale translated the New Testament into English. For his efforts, he was rewarded with exile, poverty, and persecution. Finally, in 1536, he was strangled and burned at the stake.

Don't make the mistake of assuming that your obedience to Christ will make life easier. If your conduct is pleasing to the Lord, you are very likely to suffer the world's wrath. So, rather than complain about injustice, remain steadfast in obedience and gladly wear those scars of affliction. They are like badges of honor.

JOHN 15:24, 26

"If I had not done among them the works which no one else did, they
would have no sin; but now they have seen and also hated both Me and
My Father. . . . But when the Helper comes, whom I shall send to you
from the Father, the Spirit of truth who proceeds from the Father, He
will testify of Me."

Human religion consists of manmade rules that serve a manmade god. Such religion benefits no one except those who make up the rules. That's why the religious elite in Jerusalem hated Jesus so much. He was a threat to their power. They despised the doctrine of grace He stood for, spurned the repentance He demanded, looked with disdain upon the forgiveness He offered, and repudiated the faith He epitomized. Ironically, everything He taught discredited their self-proclaimed authority to speak for God.

Because we are fallen creatures, it is all too easy to become guilty of the same hypocrisy, exchanging the true worship of God for power, money, or self-righteousness. We need to guard our hearts and minds against those tendencies and let the Word of God be a constant corrective to all that is wrong in our walk.

PHILIPPIANS 4:13

I can do all things through Christ who strengthens me.

What qualified the men Jesus chose to be His apostles? Obviously it was not any intrinsic ability or outstanding talent of their own. They were Galileans, widely regarded as low-class, rural, uneducated people. Commoners. Nobodies. Fortunately, Jesus takes great delight in accomplishing extraordinary things through ordinary people. By the time the last apostle, John, died around AD 95, churches dotted the Roman Empire from Babylon to Britain and the good news had been taken to Africa and East Asia.

Perhaps you have no celebrated talent or exceptional skill and think the important work of God's kingdom is reserved for other, more gifted people. But God still chooses "the foolish things of the world to put to shame the wise, and God has chosen the weak things of the world to put to shame the things which are mighty" (1 Corinthians 1:27). No quality shines brighter in His kingdom than humility, and no qualification ranks higher than readiness to serve. Look around you. What needs to be done that no one else is doing? The Lord is able. Are you willing?

JOHN 21:17

[Jesus] said to him the third time, "Simon, son of Jonah, do you love Me?"
Peter was grieved because He said to him the third time, "Do you love Me?"
And he said to Him, "Lord, You know all things; You know that I love
You." Jesus said to him, "Feed My sheep."

Many Christians become discouraged and disheartened when their spiritual life and witness suffer because of sin or failure. Satan may even attempt to convince us that our shortcomings render us useless to God and to His church. We tend to think we're worthless nobodies—and left to ourselves, that would be true!

Peter's dismal failure during Christ's trials stripped him of any confidence in his ability to lead God's people. He gave up the dream of becoming a "fisher of men" and returned to catching fish. And it was a wise decision from our earth-bound perspective. But to God, Peter was finally ready to serve. Stripped of pride and emptied of self-confidence, the once brash disciple would have to depend wholly upon His Lord.

If you love the Son but doubt your qualifications, you're an ideal candidate to serve Him.

1 CORINTHIANS 1:20–21

Where is the wise? Where is the scribe? Where is the disputer of this age?
Has not God made foolish the wisdom of this world? For since, in the
wisdom of God, the world through wisdom did not know God, it pleased God
through the foolishness of the message preached to save those who believe.

The apostles properly hold an exalted place in redemptive history. They are certainly worthy of their heroic place in Christian history. So let's not underestimate the importance of their office or the integrity with which they fulfilled their roles. They were the ones to whom the good news was first entrusted. They represented the true Israel of God—a genuinely repentant and believing Israel. Those truths are heightened, not diminished, by the fact that these men were so ordinary. They *became* great spiritual leaders and great preachers under the power of the Holy Spirit. And their influence is owing to one thing and one thing only: the power of the message they preached.

The time of the apostles has passed, but we have access to the same power that made them great. The Holy Spirit is promised to all who believe, and He will be faithful to transform us after the likeness of the Son—the true definition of greatness.

LUKE 6:12–13

Now it came to pass in those days that He went out to the mountain to pray, and continued all night in prayer to God. And when it was day, He called His disciples to Himself; and from them He chose twelve whom He also named apostles.

Jesus called His apostles using a two-step process. Before they could be sent out to preach, they had to be pulled in. In fact, it isn't until Luke 9:1 that Jesus gave the Twelve any authority or power. First, He identified and appointed them and brought them under His direct and personal tutelage ("that they might be with Him"). Only after several months of training did He "send them out to preach."

I've noticed that some modern-day disciples never want to leave their study rooms or prayer closets, while others are more than willing to tackle ministry on an empty spiritual tank. Yet both aspects of discipleship are essential. Wise disciples maintain a balance between time with the Master and ministry to others in His name.

What about you? Which aspect of discipleship do you tend to neglect—time at the Master's feet or work in His service? Ask your pastor or another spiritual leader to suggest practical ways you might become a more complete disciple.

LUKE 9:57–58

Now it happened as they journeyed on the road, that someone said to Him, "Lord, I will follow You wherever You go." And Jesus said to him, "Foxes have holes and birds of the air have nests, but the Son of Man has nowhere to lay His head."

The training of the apostles followed a natural progression. First, they simply followed Jesus, gleaning from His sermons and learning from His instructions along with a larger group of disciples. Next, He called them to leave everything and follow Him exclusively. Then He selected twelve men out of that group of full-time disciples, identified them as apostles, and began to focus most of His energies on their personal instruction. Later He delegated his miracle power to cast out demons and heal diseases. Finally, He sent them out, first on short-term assignments and ultimately with the command, "Go and make disciples" (Matthew 28:19).

While the Lord demands complete devotion without reservation, He is not unaware of the cost of discipleship. Nor is He uncaring. Follow Him with all your heart, mind, and strength, and trust that He will never challenge you without equipping you or send you without joining you.

LUKE 18:28–30

Then Peter said, "See, we have left all and followed You." So He said to them, "Assuredly, I say to you, there is no one who has left house or parents or brothers or wife or children, for the sake of the kingdom of God, who shall not receive many times more in this present time, and in the age to come eternal life."

Peter's words were actually a plea. He asked, in effect, "What's going to happen to us?" But the disciples had not left anything the Lord would not more than make up to them. And God did bless them in their lifetimes, despite the fact they were martyred for the sake of the gospel. He blessed them through the founding and growth of the church. They not only gained influence, respect, and honor among the people of God; but they gained multitudes of spiritual children and brothers and sisters as believers multiplied. And they will be greatly honored in the age to come.

The "cost" of discipleship is really an investment: a short-term sacrifice for the sake of long-term gain. Moreover, the call of discipleship is an invitation to exchange fleeting and mundane niceties of this world for that which truly satisfies the human soul: intimacy with God.

HEBREWS 13:7

Remember those who rule over you, who have spoken the word of God to you, whose faith follow, considering the outcome of their conduct.

When the disciples forsook their jobs, they by no means became idle. They became full-time students. For the next eighteen months they had the example of Christ perpetually before them. They could listen to His teaching, ask Him questions, watch how He dealt with people, and enjoy intimate fellowship with Him in every kind of setting. This is how the best learning occurs. It isn't just information passed on; it's one life invested in another.

The apostles were charged with the responsibility to "make disciples" (Matthew 28:19), not by founding schools (which are fine for their purpose), or by establishing courses of study (which can be very helpful), but by investing in others as Jesus had invested in them. Teaching by living, up close and personal.

You should be involved in discipleship too—both as a learner and as a teacher. Find someone who knows more than you do and learn from that person. Also find someone who knows less than you do and help teach that person.

LUKE 24:25–27

Then He said to them, "O foolish ones, and slow of heart to believe in all that the prophets have spoken! Ought not the Christ to have suffered these things and to enter into His glory?" And beginning at Moses and all the Prophets, He expounded to them in all the Scriptures the things concerning Himself.

The followers of Jesus could be amazingly thickheaded. Why was the learning process so difficult for the Twelve and His other disciples? First of all, they lacked spiritual understanding. They were slow to hear and slow to understand. They were at various times thick, dull, stupid, and blind. All of those terms or their equivalents are used to describe them in the New Testament. So how did Jesus remedy their lack of spiritual understanding? He just kept teaching. Even after His resurrection, He stayed forty days on earth "speaking of the things pertaining to the kingdom of God" (Acts 1:3).

If you struggle to understand some of the deeper truths of Scripture, you're in good company. The disciples showed the same kind of promise! Fortunately, we have a patient Master who will stop at nothing to teach us what we need to know. And He delights to take us ever deeper into the mysteries of His grace. Keep following; He'll keep teaching.

MARK 2:15

Now it happened, as He was dining in Levi's house, that many tax collectors and sinners also sat together with Jesus and His disciples; for there were many, and they followed Him.

The Twelve were an amazingly varied group. Their personalities, interests, and occupations swept the spectrum. Four were fishermen, one a tax collector, another a political activist. And they all had vastly differing personalities. Peter was eager, aggressive, bold, and outspoken, while John, his closest friend, spoke very little. Nathanael was quick to believe, while Thomas consistently wanted tangible proof throughout Christ's earthly ministry.

The Lord doesn't want mass-produced disciples off an assembly line. He wants followers of all races, vocations, social classes, personality types, and interests. He wants variety in His kingdom because the human race reflects His creative range.

Perhaps you don't fit the stereotypical mold of a Christ-follower (whatever that looks like). Good! Don't change a thing, unless it's immoral, unhealthy, or obnoxious. Whether you stand out in a crowd or blend in with the scenery, the Lord wants you with Him. And who knows? You may be surprised to discover how your uniqueness becomes an unexpected benefit for His kingdom.

LUKE 5:31–32

Jesus answered and said to them, "Those who are well have no need of a physician, but those who are sick. I have not come to call the righteous, but sinners, to repentance."

Matthew, the former tax collector (who was sometimes called Levi), was considered one of the most despicable people in Israel before Jesus called him. He had taken a job with the Roman government to extort taxes from his own people—and that tax money went to pay for the Roman occupation army. To make matters worse, tax collectors commonly took more money than the Romans required and lined their pockets with the difference. So, the fact that Jesus dined with tax collectors, and even chose one of them to join his inner circle of disciples, did not sit well with the religious elite.

Does something in your past cause you to doubt your worthiness to be a disciple of Jesus? If so, you're exactly the kind of disciple He sought, found, saved, trained, and then appointed to represent Him. His grace gives you all the "qualification" you need to become an extraordinary asset in the cause of Christ.

1 JOHN 4:7−8

Beloved, let us love one another, for love is of God; and everyone who loves is born of God and knows God. He who does not love does not know God, for God is love.

Jesus' choice of men to become His inner twelve students could have been disastrous. In addition to Matthew the tax collector, Jesus called Simon "the Zealot." Zealots were members of a loosely organized group of political extremists who often used terror and even assassination to advance their agenda: to rid their country of Romans and anyone who helped them— including tax collectors. The fact that Matthew and Simon could become part of the same company of twelve apostles is a testimony to the life-changing power and grace of Christ.

But one of the signs of true faith is this: "We know that we have passed from death to life, because we love the brethren" (1 John 3:14). Being one with Christ makes us one with all kinds of people—sometimes even those whom we might have formerly been predisposed to hate. Have you seen evidence of that kind of love in your own life? If so, how?

1 JOHN 3:2

Beloved, now we are children of God; and it has not yet been revealed what we shall be, but we know that when He is revealed, we shall be like Him, for we shall see Him as He is.

By nature, Simon Peter was brash, vacillating, and undependable. He tended to make promises he couldn't follow through with and appeared to lunge wholeheartedly into something only to bail out before finishing. When Jesus first met Simon, He gave him the nickname *Peter*, which means "Rock." It appears He wanted the new name to be a perpetual reminder to him about who he *should* be. Whenever He called him Rock, the Lord was commending His student for acting the way he ought to be acting.

When the Lord calls a disciple, He not only knows who he or she is, He also knows who he or she should be—and will be. If He can make a vacillating character like Peter as stable as a rock, He can also transform our character flaws and make us stand at the very point where we would otherwise fail. Thus His strength is perfected in our weakness (2 Corinthians 12:9). Have you seen that pattern in your own spiritual growth?

For those who live according to the flesh set their minds on the things of the flesh, but those who live according to the Spirit, the things of the Spirit.

It is obvious from the gospel narratives that the apostle John knew Peter very, very well. They were lifelong friends, business associates, and neighbors. So, in the gospel penned by John, he referred to his friend fifteen times as "Simon Peter," perhaps because he continually saw both the erratic disciple and the steady apostle. Even Peter referred to himself as "Simon Peter, a bondservant and apostle of Jesus Christ" (2 Peter 1:1) after many years of strong leadership.

Disciples who are growing and developing don't allow their old natures to become a source of shame or despair, but they also remain ever aware of who they once were. Keep your mind focused on the transforming power of the Holy Spirit, but don't be surprised to see your old nature reassert itself.

ROMANS 8:27–28

Now He who searches the hearts knows what the mind of the Spirit is,
because He makes intercession for the saints according to the will of God.
And we know that all things work together for good to those who love God,
to those who are the called according to His purpose.

In the Gospels, no disciple is so frequently rebuked by the Lord as Peter; and no disciple rebukes the Lord except Peter (Matthew 16:22). No one else confessed Christ more boldly or acknowledged His lordship more explicitly; yet no other disciple ever verbally denied Christ as forcefully or as publicly as Peter did. No one is praised and blessed by Christ the way Peter was; yet Peter was also the only one Christ ever addressed as Satan.

None of Peter's actions surprised his Master, none of his failures delayed the Lord's agenda, and nothing Peter did caused Jesus to question His plan. In fact, all of Peter's experiences contributed to making him the leader Christ wanted him to be.

Disciple-making is a messy, complicated enterprise. Fortunately, the Lord is an expert. So, pursue Him relentlessly, and don't be surprised to see Him turn your failures into triumph.

ACTS 2:14

But Peter, standing up with the eleven, raised his voice and said to them,
"Men of Judea and all who dwell in Jerusalem, let this be known to you, and
heed my words."

There is an age-old debate about whether true leaders are born or made. Peter is a strong argument for the belief that leaders are born with certain innate gifts. Even during the tumultuous days of his formation as a disciple, we see the raw elements that go into the making of a true leader. Nevertheless, these elements must also be properly shaped before someone is ready to lead others.

Peter's lack of inhibition and unbridled boldness probably irritated the other eleven throughout their training, and it exasperated the Lord on more than one occasion. But after no less than three years of divine guidance and filling by the Holy Spirit, the disciple's boldness became an invaluable asset to the early church.

Perhaps you have a personality trait you find less than helpful. Have you considered presenting it to the Lord? In His hands, your "flaws" can become a marvelous gift to others.

MATTHEW 15:15

Then Peter answered and said to Him, "Explain this parable to us."

One essential quality of a leader is inquisitiveness. The best problem solvers are people who are driven by an unquenchable enthusiasm for knowing and understanding things.

In the gospel accounts, Peter asks more questions than all the other disciples combined. It was usually Peter who asked the Lord to explain His difficult sayings, pressed Him for more information, and even asked questions of the risen Christ. He always wanted to know more, to understand better.

If you find yourself asking lots of questions and challenging the teaching you receive in order to understand more, good! Continue. Don't be shy or let anyone discourage you. Your heavenly Teacher is the Author of truth, so an honest pursuit of the truth will always take you closer to Him. And as you pursue greater understanding, don't be surprised to find a number of people following close behind.

JOHN 6:67–69

Then Jesus said to the twelve, "Do you also want to go away?" But Simon Peter answered Him, "Lord, to whom shall we go? You have the words of eternal life. Also we have come to believe and know that You are the Christ, the Son of the living God."

Another essential quality of a good leader is initiative. A true leader is the kind of person who isn't satisfied with the status quo and cannot resist the urge to make things happen.

Notice that Peter not only asked questions, but he was the first to answer and the first to act upon his convictions. He was bold and decisive, which are vital characteristics of all great leaders. Sometimes he had to take a step back, undo, retract, or be rebuked. But the fact that he was always willing to grab opportunity by the throat marked him as a natural leader.

It's okay if you don't possess this or the other qualities of a leader. But do you resent these traits in others? Do you try to put ambitious people in their place? Or are you able to encourage prospective leaders to reach their full potential?

MATTHEW 14:27−29

But immediately Jesus spoke to them, saying, "Be of good cheer! It is I; do not be afraid." And Peter answered Him and said, "Lord, if it is You, command me to come to You on the water." So He said, "Come." And when Peter had come down out of the boat, he walked on the water to go to Jesus.

There's a third element of leadership we find in Peter: involvement. True leaders are never far from the action. They don't sit in the background telling everyone else what to do; they go before their followers into the fray. Jesus came to the disciples one night out in the middle of the Sea of Galilee, walking on the water in the midst of a violent storm. Who out of all the disciples jumped out of the boat? Peter. Before anyone knew what was going on, he was walking on the waves with His master.

If your role is to lead, you can't afford to be far from the action or your followers. Be involved. Know where the action is and determine to be there. And as you move in that direction, go at a pace your followers can keep.

MATTHEW 14:30-32

But when he saw that the wind was boisterous, he was afraid; and beginning to sink he cried out, saying, "Lord, save me!" And immediately Jesus stretched out His hand and caught him, and said to him, "O you of little faith, why did you doubt?" And when they got into the boat, the wind ceased.

Jesus answered, "Come." In a flash, Peter was walking the waves. But he lost his spiritual footing. His faith faltered and he quickly began to sink. But before we look at that incident and criticize Peter too harshly, let's give him credit for having faith to leave the boat in the first place. The rest of the disciples were still clinging to their seats, trying to make sure they didn't fall overboard in the storm.

Sometimes we're afraid to risk a faith-based decision because we're afraid of failure or unsure of the outcome. What if we're wrong? What if we make a mistake?

Climb out of your seat and go! Better to trust God and make a wrong move than to do nothing and play it safe. I've discovered that God will honor even blunders made in complete dependence upon Him. He will be faithful to redirect your missteps for His glory and your benefit. So get going!

LUKE 22:61–62

And the Lord turned and looked at Peter. Then Peter remembered the word of the Lord, how He had said to him, "Before the rooster crows, you will deny Me three times." So Peter went out and wept bitterly.

Unfortunately, Peter is most famous for his three-time denial of Christ when He was arrested. But again, we need to give the brash disciple his due. Standing in the courtyard outside the place of Jesus' trial, Peter was virtually alone in a position where such a temptation could snare him. Despite his fear and weakness, he couldn't abandon Christ completely. The others didn't face this test because they cowered in dark corners far removed from danger.

You are certain to find opportunity for failure in two places: where you shouldn't be and where you should be. I'm not suggesting you go looking for trouble, so stay away from places where temptation dwells. But you run the risk of failing if you're engaged in things that matter. The other disciples didn't fail like Peter, but it's hard to fail when you're doing nothing.

JOHN 21:18–19

"Most assuredly, I say to you, when you were younger, you girded yourself and walked where you wished; but when you are old, you will stretch out your hands, and another will gird you and carry you where you do not wish." This He spoke, signifying by what death he would glorify God. And when He had spoken this, He said to him, "Follow Me."

Insatiable inquisitiveness. Enthusiastic initiative. Passionate involvement. Peter possessed the essential qualities necessary to become a great leader, but it was up to the Lord to train and shape him, because frankly, that kind of raw material, if not submitted to the Lord's control, can be downright dangerous. So the Lord dragged Peter through three years of tests and difficulties to give him a lifetime of experiences, seasoning that would turn the disciple's natural aptitude into supernatural ability.

You may or may not realize it, but you too have natural abilities. You have qualities that could produce remarkable good in the lives of everyone—if honed by God-ordained experience. That process will certainly require some challenging tests and stressful difficulties. So, disciple-in-training, be encouraged when trials come. The Lord has determined to turn your good into great!

MATTHEW 16:16-18

Simon Peter answered and said, "You are the Christ, the Son of the living God." Jesus answered and said to him, "Blessed are you, Simon Bar-Jonah, for flesh and blood has not revealed this to you, but My Father who is in heaven. And I also say to you that you are Peter, and on this rock I will build My church, and the gates of Hades shall not prevail against it."

Peter learned a lot through hard experiences. He learned, for example, that crushing defeat and deep humiliation often follow hard on the heels of our greatest victories. Just after Christ commended him for his monumental confession in Matthew 16:16, Peter suffered the harshest rebuke ever recorded of a disciple in the New Testament.

It's easier to remain humbly submitted to the Lord when we're straining under the weight of adversity. During those difficult times, we know we need Him. There's no question our life rests in His capable hands. However, when we're gliding on the wings of success, prosperity, notoriety, comfort, or good health, how quickly we take the credit and how far we are likely to plummet!

Enjoy the blessings God sends your way. Celebrate the good things that come into your life. But beware the fall that certainly follows pride. Knowing you are in the greatest danger when things are going well, humble yourself and stay closer to the Lord than ever.

MATTHEW 16:21−22

From that time Jesus began to show to His disciples that He must go to Jerusalem, and suffer many things from the elders and chief priests and scribes, and be killed, and be raised the third day. Then Peter took Him aside and began to rebuke Him, saying, "Far be it from You, Lord; this shall not happen to You!"

Jesus announced to the disciples that He was going to Jerusalem, where He would be turned over to the chief priests and scribes and be killed. Upon hearing that, Peter took Him aside for a private conference in which he denounced the Lord's plan as counterproductive to his own. Peter's perspective is perfectly understandable, if the anointed King of Israel needed political advice. But, without realizing it, he was trying to dissuade Christ from the very thing He came to earth to do.

The Lord's way might not appear consistent with good sense, but His ways are not our ways. His perspective takes eternity into account, whereas we can only guess what might occur tomorrow. His values are kingdom values, while we treasure personal comfort above all else. So rather than asking the Lord to grant us our wishes, we would do better to ask Him His.

MATTHEW 16:18–19

"And I also say to you that you are Peter, and on this rock I will build My church, and the gates of Hades shall not prevail against it. And I will give you the keys of the kingdom of heaven, and whatever you bind on earth will be bound in heaven, and whatever you loose on earth will be loosed in heaven."

Peter learned the hard way that God would reveal truth to him and guide his speech as he submitted his mind to the truth. He wasn't to depend upon a worldly wise message, but to proclaim the message given to him by God. He would also be given the keys to the kingdom—meaning that his life and message would be unlocking the kingdom of God for the salvation of many.

No true servant of God—not even an apostle—stands upon his or her own authority. The only authority we can claim is the Word we faithfully proclaim. And this, fellow disciples, allows us to wield unimaginable power, the power to unlock the gates of heaven for those around us who would receive it.

Do you regularly submit your mind to the truth of Scripture? Are you reflecting its authority by allowing God's Word to transform your thinking?

PHILIPPIANS 4:8

Finally, brethren, whatever things are true, whatever things are noble,
whatever things are just, whatever things are pure, whatever things are lovely,
whatever things are of good report, if there is any virtue and if there is
anything praiseworthy—meditate on these things.

Through the painful experience of being rebuked by the Lord, Peter learned that he was vulnerable to Satan. Satan could place words in his mouth just as surely as the Lord could. If Peter minded the things of men rather than the things of God, or if he did not do the will of God, he could be an instrument of the enemy.

Take a few moments to review the last several days. How much of that time were you exposed to the world's way of thinking? How much time with television, radio, movies, magazines, the workplace? Compare that to the time you spent in the Word, in the presence of godly friends or family, or listening to enriching music.

We can't avoid contact with the world, nor should we. However, we can be deliberate about balancing the unconstructive input we constantly receive with something good to nourish our souls. Otherwise, it will be like the old computer programmer's motto: "Garbage in, garbage out!"

LUKE 22:31–32

And the Lord said, "Simon, Simon! Indeed, Satan has asked for you, that he may sift you as wheat. But I have prayed for you, that your faith should not fail; and when you have returned to Me, strengthen your brethren."

On the eve of Christ's crucifixion, Peter fell victim to Satan again. This time he learned the hard way that he was humanly weak and could not trust his own resolve. After declaring that he would *never* deny Christ, he denied Him anyway, and he punctuated his denials with passionate curses. Thus Peter learned how watchful and careful he must be to rely upon the Lord's strength.

I know very few people who don't want to do what is right and who don't want to remain consistently faithful. Unfortunately, most fail because they mistakenly believe that success can be had by simply trying harder. The secret to success in the spiritual life—unlike business or sports—is admitting our utter helplessness and asking the Spirit of Christ to live through us.

In what area of your life do you feel most competent? Invite the Lord to show you His way, and then watch for unexpected lessons.

JOHN 1:47

Jesus saw Nathanael coming to Him, and said of him, "Behold, an Israelite indeed, in whom there is no deceit!"

Character, of course, is absolutely critical to leadership. In recent years, some have tried to argue that character doesn't really matter in leadership; what a person does in his private life supposedly should not be a factor in whether he or she is deemed fit for a public leadership role. However, time and truth go hand in hand. Leaders without character eventually disappoint their followers. True leaders, on the other hand, know that character earns respect, respect wins trust, and trust motivates followers.

Do you trust your leader's integrity enough to follow his or her directives without having to know every detail behind them? If not, why do you remain under that authority? If you trust your leader, do you lend your complete support? If you are a leader, are your unseen activities above reproach? Would you follow someone with your character?

1 CORINTHIANS 11:1

"Imitate me, just as I also imitate Christ."

Obviously, in spiritual leadership, the great goal and objective is to bring people to Christlikeness. That is why the leader himself must manifest Christlike character, which explains why the standard for leadership in the church must be set so high. The apostle Paul summarized the spirit of the true leader when he wrote, "Imitate me, just as I also imitate Christ" (1 Corinthians 11:1). Of course, Peter might just as well have written the same thing. His character was molded and shaped after the example he had witnessed in Christ.

Your leadership may or may not be in a church; regardless, you are a spiritual leader to someone. It could be your mate, your children, a coworker, or even a neighbor. No matter. The job is yours. And as a spiritual leader, your primary duty is to follow Christ.

1 Peter 2:11–12

Beloved, I urge you as aliens and strangers to abstain from fleshly lusts which wage war against the soul. Keep your behavior excellent among the Gentiles, so that in the thing in which they slander you as evildoers, they may because of your good deeds, as they observe them, glorify God in the day of visitation.

J.R. Miller wrote, "The only thing that walks back from the tomb with the mourners and refuses to be buried is the character of a man. What a man is survives him. It can never be buried." While that statement is true, there is something more important than what people think of us after we die: It's the impact we have on others for the sake of Christ while we live.

As you go through life—earning an honest wage, keeping your word, returning good for evil, regarding others more important than yourself—continually give Jesus Christ the credit. Let His glory shine so bright that when your days on earth are done, your loved ones will say, "What a great God this disciple served!"

ROMANS 13:7–8

Render therefore to all their due: taxes to whom taxes are due, customs to whom customs, fear to whom fear, honor to whom honor. Owe no one anything except to love one another, for he who loves another has fulfilled the law.

Leaders tend to be confident and aggressive, and Peter had that tendency in him. To balance this quality, the Lord taught him submission using the temple tax as an illustration.

"What do you think, Simon? From whom do the kings of the earth take customs or taxes, from their sons or from strangers?" Peter said to Him, "From strangers" (Matthew 17:25–26). In other words, kings don't tax their own children. Because Jesus is the Son of God, He was not technically obligated to pay the temple tax. Nevertheless, lest they "offend" (that is, "cause them to stumble"), He instructed Peter, "Go to the sea, cast in a hook, and take the fish that comes up first. And when you have opened its mouth, you will find a piece of money; take that and give it to them for Me and you" (17:27).

To teach Peter submission, Jesus modeled submission, which is an act of faith the Father will always honor.

ROMANS 13:1–2

Let every soul be subject to the governing authorities. For there is no
authority except from God, and the authorities that exist are appointed by
God. Therefore whoever resists the authority resists the ordinance of God,
and those who resist will bring judgment on themselves.

One of the character qualities of a spiritual leader that developed within Peter was submission. At first glance, that may seem an unusual quality to cultivate in a leader. After all, the leader is the person in charge, and he expects other people to submit to him, right? But a true leader doesn't merely demand submission; he is an example of submission by the way he submits to the Lord and to those in authority over him. Everything a true leader does ought to be marked by submission to every legitimate authority—especially submission to God and to His Word.

What kind of example do you set for those who follow you? Do you complain about poor management, or do you encourage others to honor and respect your leaders? Do you follow willingly, or do you drag your feet? How you treat your leaders is very likely how your followers treat you! Are you encouraged by that news?

1 PETER 2:18-19

Servants, be submissive to your masters with all fear, not only to the good and gentle, but also to the harsh. For this is commendable, if because of conscience toward God one endures grief, suffering wrongfully.

Christ supernaturally directed a fish that had swallowed a coin to take the bait on Peter's hook. If Jesus was Lord over nature to such a degree, He certainly had authority to opt out of the temple tax. And yet he taught Peter by example how to submit willingly.

Peter learned the lesson well. Years later he would write, "For this is the will of God, that by doing good you may put to silence the ignorance of foolish men—as free, yet not using liberty as a cloak for vice, but as bondservants of God. Honor all people. Love the brotherhood. Fear God. Honor the king" (1 Peter 2:15–17).

1 PETER 2:21–23

For to this you were called, because Christ also suffered for us, leaving us an example, that you should follow His steps: "Who committed no sin, nor was deceit found in His mouth"; who, when He was reviled, did not revile in return; when He suffered, He did not threaten, but committed Himself to Him who judges righteously.

Most people with innate leadership abilities do not naturally excel when it comes to exercising restraint, and Peter was no exception. During Jesus' arrest, Peter tried to decapitate the high priest's servant, even when surrounded by hundreds of Roman soldiers, all armed to the teeth. Fortunately, the man lost nothing but an ear, which Jesus quickly restored. Then came the rebuke. "Put your sword in its place, for all who take the sword will perish by the sword. Or do you think that I cannot now pray to My Father, and He will provide Me with more than twelve legions of angels?" (Matthew 26:52–53).

Without losing the essential qualities of boldness and courage, all leaders must cultivate self-control, discipline, moderation, and reserve. To learn how, they should learn by the example of Jesus. He had a mission to accomplish, and he never sacrificed his long-term objectives for short-term satisfaction.

MATTHEW 23:11–12

"But he who is greatest among you shall be your servant. And whoever
exalts himself will be humbled, and he who humbles himself will be exalted."

L eaders are often tempted by the sin of pride. And we can observe in Peter a tremendous amount of self-confidence. When Jesus foretold that His disciples would forsake Him, Peter said, "Even if all are made to stumble because of You, I will never be made to stumble" (Matthew 26:33). "I am ready to go with You, both to prison and to death" (Luke 22:33). Of course, we know how that turned out.

The Lord used Peter's denial to teach him humility. Later, he wrote to the churches, "Be submissive to one another, and be clothed with humility, for 'God resists the proud, but gives grace to the humble'" (1 Peter 5:5).

If you are stronger, smarter, or more gifted than most, take a lesson from Peter. Make yourself accountable to others and ask them to be brutally honest with you. Their words may hurt, but perhaps less than falling on your face.

LUKE 22:25-26

And He said to them, "The kings of the Gentiles exercise lordship over them, and those who exercise authority over them are called 'benefactors.' But not so among you; on the contrary, he who is greatest among you, let him be as the younger, and he who governs as he who serves."

In the Upper Room, sometime after Judas left, Jesus commanded the remaining eleven, "Love one another, as I have loved you. . . . By this all will know that you are My disciples, if you love one another." Not long before, Jesus showed the disciples just how they were to express love. He took on the role of a lowly servant and washed the disciples' grimy feet, even as they argued about who was the greatest among them.

It's hard for most leaders to stoop and wash the feet of those whom they perceive as subordinates. But that was the example of leadership Jesus gave, and He urged His disciples to follow it.

Washing someone's feet was the task of the lowest ranking servant in the house. What is the job no one wants in your organization? Are you willing to do it without notice or recognition? If so, you might be leadership material!

JOHN 13:13–15

"You call Me Teacher and Lord, and you say well, for so I am. If I then, your Lord and Teacher, have washed your feet, you also ought to wash one another's feet. For I have given you an example, that you should do as I have done to you."

Did Peter learn to love? He certainly did. Love became one of the hallmarks of his teaching. He encouraged the churches, "Above all things have fervent love for one another, for 'love will cover a multitude of sins'" (1 Peter 4:8). The Greek word for "fervent" literally means "stretched to the limit." Peter was urging us to love to the maximum of our capacity. The love he spoke of is not a feeling, or even how we respond to people who are lovable. This sort of love washes a brother's dirty feet. Peter himself had learned from Christ's example.

This quality made Peter a particularly effective leader. Leaders must love their followers by serving them in humility. Today as you pray, ask the Lord to bring you an opportunity to serve someone you lead in a surprising, stretched-to-the-limit way.

2 CORINTHIANS 1:3−4

Blessed be the God and Father of our Lord Jesus Christ, the Father of mercies and God of all comfort, who comforts us in all our tribulation, that we may be able to comfort those who are in any trouble, with the comfort with which we ourselves are comforted by God.

Another important character quality Peter needed to learn was *compassion*. After Peter's boast that he would never deny his Master, the Lord said, in effect, "I'm going to let Satan sift you as wheat; he will shake you to the foundations of your life and then toss you into the wind until there's nothing left but the reality of your faith" (Luke 22:31). He then reassured His disciple. "I have prayed for you that your faith should not fail; and when you have returned to Me, strengthen your brethren" (22:32).

After the sifting was complete, Peter was equipped to strengthen the brethren. He learned compassion through his ordeal so that he could comfort and strengthen others in theirs.

If you are enduring a trial, rest assured that Satan will not win; the Lord is preparing you to be a comfort for another. In the meantime, God has prepared someone to help you. Who might it be?

1 PETER 5:8–9

Be sober, be vigilant; because your adversary the devil walks about like a roaring lion, seeking whom he may devour. Resist him, steadfast in the faith, knowing that the same sufferings are experienced by your brotherhood in the world.

After the Lord restored Peter and for the rest of his life, the lead apostle would show compassion to people who were struggling. He could hardly help having great compassion for those who succumbed to temptation or fell into sin. He had been there. He could write from his own experience, "May the God of all grace, who called us to His eternal glory by Christ Jesus, after you have suffered a while, perfect, establish, strengthen, and settle you" (1 Peter 5:10).

Transparency can be your greatest asset when leading others. Consider how your failures have prepared you for leadership and how your hard-earned lessons can be an encouragement to the people God has placed in your life. Follow the example of Peter. Open the book of your life and allow others to glean wisdom from your story.

ACTS 5:28-29

"Did we not strictly command you not to teach in this name? And look, you have filled Jerusalem with your doctrine, and intend to bring this Man's blood on us!" But Peter and the other apostles answered and said: "We ought to obey God rather than men."

Leaders need courage, and so it was with Peter. However, courage is not the impetuous, headlong audacity that caused Peter to wade into a cohort of soldiers swinging a sword! He needed a mature, settled, intrepid willingness to suffer for Christ's sake. And you can practically see the birth of real courage in Peter's heart at Pentecost, when he was filled and empowered by the Holy Spirit. Acts 4 then describes how Peter and John were brought before the Jewish ruling counsel and instructed "not to speak at all nor teach in the name of Jesus" (v. 18). They boldly replied, "Whether it is right in the sight of God to listen to you more than to God, you judge. For we cannot but speak the things which we have seen and heard" (vv. 19–20). Now, *that's* courage!

The world rewards truth-tellers with persecution. Those who lead must stand upon truth, for they have no other authority. Therefore, ill treatment is the occupational hazard of the leader. If you ask God for anything, ask Him for courage. You'll need it.

1 PETER 1:3-4

Blessed be the God and Father of our Lord Jesus Christ, who according to His abundant mercy has begotten us again to a living hope through the resurrection of Jesus Christ from the dead, to an inheritance incorruptible and undefiled and that does not fade away, reserved in heaven for you.

After Peter's training and subsequent trials, he was secure in Christ. He had seen the risen Christ, so he knew Christ had conquered death. He knew whatever earthly trials came his way, they were merely temporary. The trials, though often painful and always distasteful, were nothing compared to the hope of eternal glory. That hope is what gave Peter such courage.

We must be careful to place our hope in what is certain. We often hope to avoid trials or hope that godly decisions will not reap unpleasant consequences, but that is not what Christ has promised. In fact, He assured us we would suffer just as He suffered (John 15:18–21). Instead, we must cling to the promise He did make, that no trial would overcome us, that trials would redound to His glory, and that we will eventually share in that glory.

Genuine courage can come only from this hope, and leaders need steady doses of it.

JOHN 1:42

[Andrew] brought [Simon] to Jesus. Now when Jesus looked at him, He said, "You are Simon the son of Jonah. You shall be called Cephas" (which is translated, A Stone).

The Lord's training program for Peter transformed his character. As he became the man Christ wanted him to be, he gradually changed from Simon into Rock. He learned submission, restraint, humility, love, compassion, and courage from the Lord's example. And because of the Holy Spirit's work in his heart, he became a great leader. He preached to thousands (Acts 2:14–41), he healed the hopeless (3:1–10), he raised the dead (9:36–42), he took the gospel to the Gentiles (Acts 10), and he wrote two epistles. What a disciple! What a leader!

Of the twelve, this vacillating, impetuous, boastful, emotional loose cannon was perhaps the least likely man to become a stabilizing force in the early church. But God sees people differently than we do. Nothing and no one can keep Him from accomplishing His purposes.

Take a few moments to review your past and to trace your path to this point in your life. What does the Lord appear to be doing, and to what role do you imagine it leading?

ACTS 10:28

Then he said to [the assembled Gentiles], "You know how unlawful it is for a Jewish man to keep company with or go to one of another nation. But God has shown me that I should not call any man common or unclean."

P eter became a remarkable force for good in the early church, but he was not perfect. In Galatians 2, we see a brief flash of the old Simon, who was eating with Gentiles until some false teachers from among the Jews showed up. These heretics insisted that Gentiles could not be saved unless they came to the Messiah through the door of the Law. Peter, apparently intimidated by the false teachers, stopped eating with his Gentile brethren (v.12).

Paul rebuked Peter openly and, to Peter's credit, he responded to Paul's correction with repentance. And when the matter came before all the leaders in Jerusalem, Peter was the first to speak in defense of the gospel of pure grace (Acts 15:7–14). Peter remained teachable, humble, and sensitive to the Holy Spirit's conviction and correction.

No one expects disciples or leaders to be perfect. However, everyone respects those who can admit their faults, acknowledge their weaknesses, and accept correction with dignity. May all our leaders be so great.

2 PETER 3:18

Grow in the grace and knowledge of our Lord and Savior Jesus Christ. To Him be the glory both now and forever. Amen.

How did Peter's life end? We know that Jesus told Peter he would die as a martyr (John 21:18–19). But Scripture doesn't record the death of Peter. The church historian Eusebius cites the testimony of Clement, who says that before Peter was crucified he was forced to watch the crucifixion of his wife. As he watched her being led to her death, Clement says Peter called to her by name, saying "Remember the Lord." Peter then pleaded to be crucified upside down because he wasn't worthy to die as his Lord had died. And thus he was nailed to a cross head-down.

Peter would not have regarded this as a tragic end but as a glorious fulfillment of Christ's Word. This was a destiny for which he undoubtedly prepared himself for many years. And that is exactly why he became Rock—the great leader of the early church.

GENESIS 3:20

Adam called his wife's name Eve, because she was the mother of all living.

E ve must have been a creature of unsurpassed beauty. She was the crown and pinnacle of God's amazing creative work. The first female human was fashioned directly by the Creator's hand in a way that showed particular care and attention to detail. Remember, Eve wasn't made out of dust like Adam, but carefully designed from living flesh and bone. Adam was refined dirt; Eve was a glorious refinement of humanity itself. She was a special gift to Adam, the necessary partner who completed the reflection of God's image in humanity. Her advent signaled the completion of all creation.

Some critics have accused the Bible and Christianity for devaluing women, but a fair reading of Scripture would prove otherwise. Scripture exalts faithful women and their role. The Lord's tender fondness for women is undeniable, which is wonderfully illustrated in His creation of the first.

1 PETER 3:7

*Husbands, likewise, dwell with [women] with understanding, giving honor
to the wife, as to the weaker vessel, and as being heirs together of the grace of
life, that your prayers may not be hindered.*

Nothing in the whole expanse of the universe was more wonderful than this woman made from a handful of Adam. If
the man represented the supreme species (a race of creatures
made in the image of God), Eve was the living embodiment of
humanity's glory. God had truly saved the best for last. Nothing
else would have sufficed quite so perfectly to be the finishing
touch and the very zenith of all creation.

If Eve is the supreme example of womanhood as God originally
intended, then the honor God gives her is the model for how all
women should be treated. In fact, the Lord appears to have little
patience with men who do not honor their wives.

I SAMUEL 16:7

"The LORD does not see as man sees; for man looks at the outward
appearance, but the LORD looks at the heart."

S cripture gives us no physical description of Eve. Her beauty—
splendid as it must have been—is never mentioned or even
alluded to. The focus of the biblical account is on Eve's duty to
her Creator and her role alongside her husband. That is a significant fact, reminding us that the chief distinguishing traits of
true feminine excellence are nothing superficial. People who are
obsessed with image, cosmetics, body shapes, and other external
matters have a distorted view of femininity. Indeed, Western culture as a whole (including a large segment of the visible church)
seems hopelessly confused about these very issues.

We need to go back to Scripture to see what God's ideal for a
woman really is. A quick study of Eve reveals that God's ideal
woman—like His ideal man—is a person of godly character.

GENESIS 2:22–23

Then the rib which the LORD God had taken from man He made into a woman, and He brought her to the man. And Adam said: "This is now bone of my bones and flesh of my flesh; she shall be called Woman, because she was taken out of Man."

Although Scripture is silent about many things we might like to know about Eve, we are given detailed accounts of her creation, her temptation and fall, the curse that was placed on her, and the subsequent hope that she clung to. Not surprisingly, they are much the same details we have of Adam; however, the subtle differences in their experience tell us a great deal about Eve, and therefore womanhood after the Fall.

Women and men are alike in so many ways, yet our subtle differences profoundly affect how we experience the joys, sorrows, victories, and failures of life. Our perspectives and perceptions are different. The roles we were designed to fulfill are different. Neither gender is superior or inferior to the other—but they are clearly *different.* God designed it this way, and He makes no mistakes, so both are essential, and each must fulfill the proper God-ordained role. They complement and balance one another perfectly.

GENESIS 2:24–25

Therefore a man shall leave his father and mother and be joined to his wife, and they shall become one flesh. And they were both naked, the man and his wife, and were not ashamed.

The Hebrew expression describing how God "made [the rib] into a woman" denotes careful construction and detailed forethought. Literally, it means God *built* a woman. He carefully crafted a whole new creature with just the right set of attributes to make her the ideal mate for Adam, and therefore Adam was ideal for her. The Hebrew phrase translated "comparable" means literally, "corresponding opposite."

When Adam awoke, he already felt a deep, personal attachment to Eve. She was a priceless treasure to be cherished, a worthy partner to encourage him, and a pleasing spouse with whom to share mutual love and support.

The creation of Eve and her union with Adam established marriage and the family as the first institutions and the essential building blocks of all human society. Marriage itself is a divine gift to the human race—to be treasured and enjoyed. That truth should be reflected constantly in the way we honor and care for one another as husband and wife.

PROVERBS 31:10–11

Who can find a virtuous wife?
For her worth is far above rubies.
The heart of her husband safely trusts her;
So he will have no lack of gain.

The unique method of Eve's creation is deliberately emphasized, I think, in order to remind us of several crucial truths about womanhood in general. First, it speaks of Eve's fundamental equality with Adam. Second, the way Eve was created illustrates God's intention for their marriage to be based on monogamy, solidarity, and inviolability. Third, the circumstances of Eve's creation illustrate how their pairing was not merely a physical union, but a union of heart and soul as well. Fourth, Eve's creation contains important biblical lessons about the divinely designed gifts of women to do what only they can.

Because marriage memorializes the original pairing of Adam and Eve, each of these truths should be a guide to those who choose this lifelong covenant. If you are married, ask your spouse to rate how well your marriage reflects each of these four principles. Let me warn you: don't expect all 10s!

GENESIS 3:1

Now the serpent was more cunning than any beast of the field which the
LORD God had made. And he said to the woman, "Has God indeed said,
'You shall not eat of every tree of the garden'?"

S atan came to Eve in disguise. That epitomizes the subtle way
he intended to deceive her. Moreover, what the serpent told
her was not only plausible; it was even partially true. Eating the
fruit would indeed open her eyes to understand good and evil. In
her innocence, Eve was susceptible to the devil's half-truths and
lies. And the serpent's opening words set the tenor for all his dealings with humanity: "Has God indeed said . . . ?" Casting doubt on
the goodness of God's character and the truth of His Word has
been Satan's modus operandi ever since.

Doubting the goodness or truthfulness of God or His Word
is a warning signal. We are dangerously close to falling when
such an attitude rises up from within. That is the time to reach
out to a mature, trusted believer and ask for some much needed
perspective.

GENESIS 2:15–17

Then the LORD God took the man and put him in the garden of Eden to tend and keep it. And the LORD God commanded the man, saying, "Of every tree of the garden you may freely eat; but of the tree of the knowledge of good and evil you shall not eat, for in the day that you eat of it you shall surely die."

In addition to casting doubt on the goodness of God, Satan twisted the meaning of God's Word: "Has God indeed said, 'You shall not eat of every tree of the garden'?" God's commandment had actually come to Adam as a positive statement, "you may freely eat," with a solitary restriction. But the serpent cast the commandment in negative language, making God's expression of lavish generosity sound like stinginess.

This glass-half-empty perspective on God's Word and God's provision lay at the root of all sorts of sin. Furthermore, the deadly deception of evil is that sin will supply what God has left lacking. God's Word, on the other hand, assures us that He knows us better than we know ourselves, and that whatever we don't have is not truly needed.

GENESIS 3:4–5

Then the serpent said to the woman, "You will not surely die. For God knows that in the day you eat of it your eyes will be opened, and you will be like God, knowing good and evil."

The second time the serpent speaks to Eve, he does not merely misquote God's Word in order to put a sinister spin on it. This time he flatly contradicts what God had told Adam. Then Satan went on to confound Eve with his version of what would happen if she ate, which contained another partial truth. Indeed, her eyes would be open to the knowledge of good and evil. But rather than gaining something of value, she would forfeit her innocence. And rather than becoming more like God, she would become less like Him! Eating the fruit would (and did) make her more like the devil—fallen, corrupt, and condemned.

The allure of sin remains the same today. It *always* promises to give, but it *always* takes away. Nevertheless, the sin-loving nature we inherit from Adam is programmed to believe the lie even as our conscience screams its warning. Our only hope is to receive a new nature, one that heeds the voice of God.

GENESIS 3:6

So when the woman saw that the tree was good for food, that it was pleasant to the eyes, and a tree desirable to make one wise, she took of its fruit and ate. She also gave to her husband with her, and he ate.

Notice the natural desires that contributed to Eve's confusion: her bodily appetites, her aesthetic sensibilities, and her intellectual curiosity. Those are all good, legitimate, healthy urges—unless the object of desire is sinful, and then natural passion becomes evil lust.

Someone described sin as choosing illegitimate fulfillment of a legitimate need. That might be an oversimplification, but there's a lot of truth in that statement. Very often the motivation for sin is a need we have chosen to fill on our own, apart from God. A better response would be to become more aware of what need we are trying to meet and then present it to God in prayer, asking Him to provide. Then, we must do something very difficult: We must *wait*. Moreover, we must accept His response with thanksgiving, even if it's perplexing at first.

The Lord is faithful, and He will always supply our needs.

1 CORINTHIANS 15:57–58

Thanks be to God, who gives us the victory through our Lord Jesus Christ.
Therefore, my beloved brethren, be steadfast, immovable, always abounding
in the work of the Lord, knowing that your labor is not in vain in the Lord.

Long after the memory of the disciples' miracles and achievements has faded, the legacy of their true greatness lives on: the church, a living, breathing organism which they helped found and of which they became the very foundation stones. The church exists today because these men launched the expansion of the gospel of Jesus Christ to the ends of the earth. And their heroism will be rewarded and commemorated throughout eternity in the New Jerusalem, where their names will be permanently etched into the foundation of that city.

Obviously God could have evangelized the world without disciples. He's omnipotent! So why does He call and empower people to do what He can do on His own? Because He loves us. He calls us to join Him as He redeems the world from evil, and when He succeeds, He will share the spoils and rewards of victory with His elect. In the end, we will cast those rewards at His feet as a way of acknowledging that all glory belongs to Him—but what a privilege it is for us to participate with Him in the outworking of His eternal plan!

GENESIS 3:6−7

So when the woman saw that the tree was good for food, that it was pleasant to the eyes, and a tree desirable to make one wise, she took of its fruit and ate. She also gave to her husband with her, and he ate. Then the eyes of both of them were opened, and they knew that they were naked; and they sewed fig leaves together and made themselves coverings.

The serpent was right about one thing: eating the forbidden fruit opened Eve's eyes so that she knew good and evil. Unfortunately, she knew evil by experiencing it—by becoming a willing participant in sin. And in a moment, her innocence was gone. The result was agonizing shame, illustrated by the first couple's pathetic attempt to cover themselves.

Of course, our coverings are no less pitiful: Human religion, philanthropy, education, self-betterment, self-esteem, and all other attempts at human goodness ultimately fail to provide adequate camouflage for the disgrace and shame of our fallen state. The kind of covering we need cannot be provided by any earthly means. We need help from above.

Genesis 3:16

To the woman He said: "I will greatly multiply your sorrow and your conception; in pain you shall bring forth children; your desire shall be for your husband, and he shall rule over you."

Paradise was utterly ruined by sin, and the gravity of the curses must have shattered Eve's heart. But God's judgment against her was not entirely harsh and hopeless. There was a good deal of grace, even in the curse. For example, Eve might have been utterly destroyed, or made to wander alone in a world where survival would have been difficult. Instead, she and Adam were permitted to remain together, for her to care for him and Adam to provide for her. In the worst case, Eve might have been forbidden to bear children. Although the experience would now be painful and accompanied by sorrow, Eve would still be the mother of all living.

The sad fact of the matter is, we all deserve much worse consequences for sin than the mere chastisement we receive. Even when the affliction of a sin-sick world makes life difficult, each day is a gift of grace. Think of where we should be!

[God said to the serpent,] "And I will put enmity between you and the woman, and between your seed and her Seed; He shall bruise your head, and you shall bruise His heel."

The promise that Eve would still bear children mitigated every other aspect of the curse. There was even a hint in the curse itself that one of Eve's own offspring would ultimately overthrow evil and dispel all the darkness of sin. Adam and Eve had set a whole world of evil in motion by their disobedience; now, through Eve's offspring, she would produce a Savior. This powerful hope had already been implicitly given to her, in the portion of the curse where the Lord addressed the serpent.

Jesus Christ is that hope; He is that Savior. He is our covering, not merely concealing shame but removing it. He is that help from above, God in human flesh, sent to live the perfect life we cannot live and to die an atoning death to pay the penalty of our sin. And through His resurrection, all those who trust in Him receive the free gift of eternal life. Are you still living under the curse when you could be covered by grace?

HEBREWS 9:27-28

It is appointed for men to die once, but after this the judgment, so Christ
was offered once to bear the sins of many. To those who eagerly wait for
Him He will appear a second time, apart from sin, for salvation.

E ve could not possibly have grasped the full scope of the divine
pledge concealed in God's curse on the serpent, but she could
hardly have failed to take heart from what she heard. She knew she
was not going to be instantly destroyed. Instead, because of God's
great grace and mercy, one of her offspring would ultimately inflict
a crushing blow to the tempter's head, utterly and finally destroying Satan and all his influence—in effect, overturning all the wickedness Eve had helped to unleash. The grace of God is indeed
amazing. Even in His chastisement, He makes a way for salvation.

What applied to Eve applies to the whole human race: although
we live in a cursed world amid all the bitter consequences of sin,
this life is not hopeless. The curse underscores the evil and
destructive consequences of sin, but it also reminds us that God
Himself provides redemption for those who trust Him. In fact, we
have an even better perspective than Eve did, because we can see
in Christ the fulfillment of the redemption she could only hope
for and wonder about.

JOHN 12:37-38

*But although He had done so many signs before them, they did not believe in
Him, that the word of Isaiah the prophet might be fulfilled, which he spoke:*
    "Lord, who has believed our report?
    And to whom has the arm of the LORD been revealed?"

The most notorious and universally scorned of all the disciples is Judas Iscariot, the betrayer. His name appears last in every biblical list of apostles, except for the list in Acts 1, where it doesn't appear at all. He is the most colossal failure in all of human history. He committed the most horrible, heinous act of any individual, ever. He betrayed the perfect, sinless, holy Son of God for a handful of money. He spent three years with Jesus Christ, but for all that time his heart was only growing hard and hateful.

It's difficult to understand how a person could be in the presence of the Lord for that amount of time and then fail to embrace Him as Savior and worship Him as God. Yet it happened in the case of Judas in the first century, and it happens to many, many others in the twenty-first. That's because belief is not an intellectual decision; it's a crisis of the will, and therefore a moral decision.

JOHN 3:10–11

Jesus answered and said to [Nicodemus], "Are you the teacher of Israel, and do not know these things? Most assuredly, I say to you, We speak what We know and testify what We have seen, and you do not receive Our witness."

The other eleven apostles are all great encouragements to us because they exemplify how common people with typical failings can be used by God in *un*common, remarkable ways. Judas, on the other hand, stands as a warning about the evil potential of spiritual carelessness, squandered opportunity, sinful lusts, and hardness of the heart. Here was a man who drew as close to the Savior as it is humanly possible to be. He enjoyed every privilege Christ affords. He was intimately familiar with everything Jesus taught. Yet he remained in unbelief and went into a hopeless eternity.

Vast religious knowledge does not necessarily bring someone closer to genuine trust in Jesus Christ and acceptance of the free gift of eternal life He offers. If the heart remains stubbornly dedicated to living on its own terms, the mind will accept any delusion Satan offers.

EPHESIANS 4:4–6

There is one body and one Spirit, just as you were called in one hope of your calling; one Lord, one faith, one baptism; one God and Father of all, who is above all, and through all, and in you all.

Judas's surname, Iscariot, signifies the region he came from. It is derived from the Hebrew term *ish* ("man") and the name of a town, Kerioth—"man of Kerioth." Judas probably came from Kerioth-hezron (cf. Joshua 15:25), a humble town in the south of Judea. He was apparently the only one of the apostles who did not come from Galilee. As we know, many of the others were brothers, friends, and working companions even before meeting Christ. Judas was a solitary figure who entered their midst from afar.

We can't read too much into Judas's different background and lack of prior association. Each of the disciples was unique in his own way and came to the group with something that could have estranged him from the rest. Ultimately, what united them was not their personal histories, but the fact that each shared a bond with Christ.

MARK 10:13–15

Then [parents] brought little children to Him, that He might touch them; but the disciples rebuked those who brought them. But when Jesus saw it, He was greatly displeased and said to them, "Let the little children come to Me, and do not forbid them; for of such is the kingdom of God. Assuredly, I say to you, whoever does not receive the kingdom of God as a little child will by no means enter it."

Judas's name is a form of *Judah*. The name means "Yahweh leads," which indicates that when he was born his parents must have had great hopes for him to be led by God. The irony of the name is that no individual was ever more clearly led by Satan than Judas was.

A godly home, a biblically sound church, a God-oriented heritage, and a good name all contribute to give a child both direction and momentum for his or her journey toward the Lord. But eventually he or she is responsible for steering away from Him. Ultimately, no one is to blame but the individual for failure to embrace the Savior, especially when he or she has been given a good start in life.

PROVERBS 26:24–25

He who hates, disguises it with his lips,
    And lays up deceit within himself;
When he speaks kindly, do not believe him,
    For there are seven abominations in his heart;
Though his hatred is covered by deceit,
    His wickedness will be revealed before the assembly.

The Galilean disciples' unfamiliarity with Judas would have aided and abetted him in his deception. The others knew little about his family, his background, or his life before he became a disciple. So it was easy for him to keep his inner life a secret and to play the hypocrite. He was able to work his way into a place of trust, which we know he did because he ultimately became the treasurer of the group and used that position to pilfer funds (John 12:6).

An imposter cannot hide his or her deceit forever. A secret self can be cultivated away from the eyes of the world for a time, but eventually the individual will become so blinded to his own darker nature that he arrogantly assumes no one else can see it either. Eventually—and this is true for all of us—our sins *will* find us out.

JEREMIAH 17:9

"The heart is deceitful above all things,
And desperately wicked;
Who can know it?"

Judas was ordinary in every way, just like the others. It is significant that when Jesus predicted one of them would betray Him, no one pointed the finger of suspicion at Judas (Matthew 26:22–23). He was so expert in his hypocrisy that no one seemed to distrust him. But Jesus knew his heart from the beginning (John 6:64).

While no one can deny the evil in Judas's heart, we run the risk of so vilifying him that we fail to identify with his humanity, and therefore fail to heed the warning signal blaring at us through his example. He was a man like any other, with a depraved, desperately wicked heart beating in his chest. But rather than confess his sin, he expertly hid it. And rather than submit it to Christ for healing and restoration, he nurtured his evil nature until it ruled him. Satan became his master as a result.

Beware! No one is immune! Fortunately, Christ knows the heart and wants to wash it clean.

PSALM 51:9−10

Hide Your face from my sins,
And blot out all my iniquities.
Create in me a clean heart, O God,
And renew a steadfast spirit within me.

The New Testament tells us plenty about Judas—enough to establish a clear fact. The life of Judas reminds us that it is possible to be near Christ and associate with His people closely (but superficially) and yet become utterly hardened in sin. He began exactly like the other disciples had begun. But he never laid hold of the truth by faith, so he was never transformed like the rest. While they were increasing in faith as sons of God, he was becoming more and more a child of hell.

The lesson we take from Judas's life is not difficult to understand. If we don't want to end up like him, we mustn't be the kind of hypocrite he was. Christ calls sinful people to repentance with the promise of cleansing and renewal. Judas pretended to follow Christ, but he never really answered Christ's call to repent.

JOHN 3:3

Jesus answered and said to [Nicodemus, the foremost teacher of religion in Israel], "Most assuredly, I say to you, unless one is born again, he cannot see the kingdom of God."

The call of Judas is not recorded in Scripture. It is obvious, however, that he followed Jesus willingly. He lived in a time of heightened messianic hope, and like most in Israel, he was eager for the Messiah to come. When he heard about Jesus, he must have become convinced that this must be the true Messiah. Like the other eleven, he left whatever other enterprise he may have been engaged in and began to follow Jesus full-time. Judas even stayed with Jesus when less devoted disciples began to leave the group (John 6:66–71). He had given his life to following Jesus. But he never gave Jesus his heart.

That's the essence of hypocrisy. Outward devotion without inward conviction. Oh, sure, we sometimes must do the right thing when we don't feel like it, but not as a way of life. Eventually, we must abandon all hope of self-help and come to Christ, asking for Him to do within us what only He can do.

MATTHEW 6:31–33

"Therefore do not worry, saying, 'What shall we eat?' or 'What shall we drink?' or 'What shall we wear?' . . . For your heavenly Father knows that you need all these things. But seek first the kingdom of God and His righteousness, and all these things shall be added to you."

Judas was probably a young, zealous, patriotic Jew who did not want the Romans to rule and who hoped Christ would overthrow the foreign oppressors and restore the kingdom to Israel. He obviously could see that Jesus had powers like no other man. There was plenty of reason for a man like Judas to be attracted to that. However, it is equally obvious that Judas was not attracted to Christ on a spiritual level. He followed Jesus out of desire for selfish gain, worldly ambition, avarice, and greed.

People turn to religion and religious institutions for all sorts of reasons. All too often, it's to enhance the lives they want for themselves, or to ward off any unseen evil that might destroy what they build. But the Messiah calls people to leave their selfish expectations behind and come to Him on His terms. This step of faith trusts that He will provide what we need and orchestrate what is best for all.

JOHN 13:18–19

"I do not speak concerning all of you. I know whom I have chosen; but that the Scripture may be fulfilled, 'He who eats bread with Me has lifted up his heel against Me.' Now I tell you before it comes, that when it does come to pass, you may believe that I am He."

It is clear, on the one hand, that Judas chose to follow. He continued following even when following became difficult. He persisted in following even though it required him to be a more clever hypocrite. On the other hand, Jesus also chose him. The tension between divine sovereignty and human choice is manifest in Judas's calling, just as it is manifest in the calling of the other disciples. But his calling was not for redemption. His role of betrayal was ordained before the foundation of the world and prophesied in Psalm 41:9. Jesus even cited that verse and said its fulfillment would come in His own betrayal.

The life and betrayal of Judas assures us that no matter how sinful a person may be, no matter what treachery he or she may attempt against God, the purpose of God cannot be thwarted. Even the worst act of treachery works toward the fulfillment of the divine plan.

GENESIS 50:19–20

Joseph said to [his treacherous brothers], "Do not be afraid, for am I in the place of God? But as for you, you meant evil against me; but God meant it for good, in order to bring it about as it is this day, to save many people alive."

Scripture affirms that when Jesus chose Judas, He knew Judas would be the one to fulfill the prophecies of betrayal. He knowingly chose him to fulfill the plan. And yet Judas was in no sense coerced into doing what he did. No invisible hand forced him to betray Christ. He acted freely and without external compulsion. He was responsible for his own actions. His own greed, his own ambition, and his own wicked desires were the only forces that constrained him to betray Christ. Judas acted on his own to perpetrate evil; God merely used his treachery to accomplish His own plan.

The same principle plays out in the life of the believer. Evil will still try to steal, kill, and destroy, but God will prevail. He will use all things, even the treachery of others and tragedy in the world, to accomplish the good He desires for us.

LUKE 22:21–22

[Jesus said,] "Behold, the hand of My betrayer is with Me on the table. And truly the Son of Man goes as it has been determined, but woe to that man by whom He is betrayed!"

How do we reconcile the fact that Judas's treachery was prophesied and predetermined with the fact that he acted of his own volition? There is no need to reconcile those two facts. They are not in contradiction. God's plan and Judas's evil deed concurred perfectly. Judas did what he did because his heart was evil. God, who works all things according to the counsel of his own will, had foreordained that Jesus would be betrayed and that He would die for the sins of the world.

I find great comfort in the fact that God does not constrain people to behave a certain way, yet nothing—not even the evil deeds of evil people—can undermine His sovereignty. I cannot explain how this can be true. Fortunately, I don't have to. I merely trust in the goodness and the wisdom and the sovereign power of God. When I reflect on His nature, I trust. And when I trust, the need for detailed answers fades, and I worship.

PSALM 32:5

I acknowledged my sin to You,
And my iniquity I have not hidden.
I said, "I will confess my transgressions to the LORD,"
And You forgave the iniquity of my sin.

Judas had every opportunity to turn from his sin—as much opportunity as was ever afforded anyone. He heard numerous appeals from Christ urging him *not* to do the deed he was planning to do. He heard every lesson Jesus taught during His ministry. Many of those lessons applied directly to him. Jesus even cautioned the Twelve, "One of you is a devil" (John 6:70). Yet Judas listened to all of that unmoved. He never applied the lessons. He just kept nurturing a secret self that he deftly kept hidden from everyone.

The danger of hidden sin is the illusion that there is no victim and there are no consequences. But sin *never* remains static. Sin thrives in dark seclusion and it always breeds greater evil. Always. The only right thing to do with sin is to bring it out of hiding through confession. Bring it to God and call it what it is. Even better is if you can do this with a trusted friend.

"Indeed before the day was, I am He;
And there is no one who can deliver out of My hand;
I work, and who will reverse it?"

J udas was becoming progressively more disillusioned with Christ. No doubt at the start, *all* the apostles thought of the Jewish Messiah as an oriental monarch who would defeat the enemies of Judea, rid Israel of pagan occupation, and reestablish the Davidic kingdom in unprecedented glory. Jesus was the obvious fulfillment of the Old Testament messianic promises. But he did not always fulfill their personal expectations and ambitions.

We all want the Christ we're looking for, and we hope He will make life what *we* want it to be. But that's not a genuine response to His call. We are invited to follow Him, which means that expecting Him to do *our* will is simply absurd. And yet . . .

What expectations have you brought to Christ that are not being fulfilled? Perhaps it's time to lay your expectations aside and ask Him to reveal His.

ISAIAH 55:8-9

"For My thoughts are not your thoughts,
Nor are your ways My ways," says the LORD.
"For as the heavens are higher than the earth,
So are My ways higher than your ways,
And My thoughts than your thoughts."

To be perfectly honest, the disciples' expectations were not all spiritually motivated. We see evidence of this from time to time, such as when James and John asked for the chief seats in the kingdom. Most of them had hoped to see an earthly, materialistic, political, military, and economic kingdom. Although they had left all to follow Jesus, they did so with an expectation that they would be rewarded. Indeed, they would, but not with cabinet positions after a successful coup. Their full and final reward would be in the age to come.

Jesus promised us abundant life, which is different from worldly wealth. He promised us eternal life, but we must pass through physical death. He promised us power, which we have through the indwelling Spirit of God. Someone who doesn't assign these blessings the same value God does will be disappointed. Eventually, eleven of the Twelve grew wise. Judas refused to see things from the Lord's perspective.

LUKE 22:28–30

[Jesus said,] "But you are those who have continued with Me in My trials. And I bestow upon you a kingdom, just as My Father bestowed one upon Me, that you may eat and drink at My table in My kingdom, and sit on thrones judging the twelve tribes of Israel."

The rest of the apostles had begun to catch on slowly that the true Messiah was not what they at first expected. They embraced the superior understanding of the biblical promises Jesus unfolded to them. Their love for Christ overcame their worldly ambitions. They received His teaching about the spiritual dimensions of the kingdom, and they gladly became partakers.

Judas, meanwhile, simply became disillusioned and hid his disappointment under his blanket of hypocrisy, probably because he was looking for a way to get some money out of the years he had invested with Jesus. He remained an outsider, albeit secretly. Greed and selfishness eventually gave way to bitterness, and in the end, Judas betrayed Christ—and in effect sold his own soul—for a sum that would not have supported him for a year. He forfeited an eternity of blessing and reward for a few coins he was not able to hold on to for more than a few hours. What a tragic figure he was!

EPHESIANS 4:26−27

"Be angry, and do not sin": do not let the sun go down on your wrath, nor give place to the devil.

By the time Jesus and the apostles went to Jerusalem for the Passover in the last year of Jesus' earthly ministry, Judas's spiritual disenfranchisement was complete. At some point in those final few days, his disillusionment turned to hate, and hate mixed with greed finally turned to treachery. Judas probably convinced himself that Jesus had stolen three years of money-making potential. That sort of thinking ate away at him until finally he became the monster who betrayed Christ.

Note that his transformation from eager disciple to greedy traitor didn't occur overnight. He nurtured his growing resentment over many months, keeping it unsafely hidden while his character steadily eroded from the inside out. That's how resentment can poison a soul. Resentment leads to hate, which then begets evil of all kinds.

Don't ignore resentment. It seems like such an insignificant, easily managed nuisance, but it gives Satan ample opportunity to begin his sinister work.

2 THESSALONIANS 2:11–12

For this reason God will send them strong delusion, that they should believe the lie, that they all may be condemned who did not believe the truth but had pleasure in unrighteousness.

Shortly after raising Lazarus from the dead, Jesus and the disciples returned to Bethany, on the outskirts of Jerusalem. At a banquet, Lazarus's sister, Mary, "took a pound of very costly oil of spikenard, anointed the feet of Jesus, and wiped His feet with her hair" (John 12:3). The act was shocking in its extravagance. Judas was indeed shocked, saying, "Why was this fragrant oil not sold for [three hundred days' wage] and given to the poor?" (v.5).

Such concern for the poor from the man who routinely pilfered ministry funds! I don't doubt that the public half of Judas actually meant what he said. Clearly the man was blinded to his own evil.

The Lord has been known to allow the self-delusion of sin to seal a person's fate and to use his or her evil to accomplish His purposes. Beware the mind-warping power of sustained sin!

MATTHEW 26:14–16

Then one of the twelve, called Judas Iscariot, went to the chief priests and said, "What are you willing to give me if I deliver Him to you?" And they counted out to him thirty pieces of silver. So from that time he sought opportunity to betray [Jesus].

After sharply rebuking Mary's lavish act of worship, Judas received a rebuke from Jesus. But he didn't repent. He didn't even examine his own heart. In fact, it appears to have been the catalyst for His betrayal. His heart seethed with a poisonous mixture of pride, resentment, greed, and ambition, and it finally boiled over when he was corrected in front of others.

A psychologist would say that Judas bottled up his anger until the pressure exploded in an act of uncontrolled destruction. John's gospel declares that Satan put it in his heart to betray Christ. Both are correct. Satan didn't *force* Judas to act; he cleverly gave Judas the opportunity to consummate the hatred he harbored against the Lord.

Make no mistake. Hatred isn't a harmless emotion. It is a means by which Satan can gain powerful influence in your life.

PROVERBS 27:5–6

Open rebuke is better
Than love carefully concealed.
Faithful are the wounds of a friend,
But the kisses of an enemy are deceitful.

Notice that this is the first time Judas had ever exposed himself in any way. Up to that point, he had blended in perfectly with the rest of the group. This is the first time on record that he merited any kind of direct rebuke. However, given the circumstances, and that Jesus knew perfectly well what was in Judas's heart, His response was remarkably mild. He could have blasted Judas with a fierce condemnation and exposed his real motives, but He didn't. Nevertheless, the gentle reprimand seems to have made Judas resent Jesus even more.

Some people simply will not tolerate correction, especially when they are prideful by nature. Even a gentle rebuke is likely to spark a nasty response.

Are you open to correction? When reproved by a loved one, do you feel attacked, or do you receive their admonition as a gift motivated by love?

LUKE 6:27–28

[Jesus said,] "But I say to you who hear: Love your enemies, do good to those who hate you, bless those who curse you, and pray for those who spitefully use you."

On the eve of His crucifixion, Jesus gave the apostles a lesson in humility by washing their feet. He washed the feet of all twelve, which means He even washed the feet of Judas. Judas sat there and let Jesus wash his feet and remained utterly unmoved. The world's worst sinner was also the world's best hypocrite. Yet that didn't stop Jesus from extending kindness to His enemy. And by washing the feet of the man who would betray Him, Jesus practiced what He had preached.

Returning good for evil will not be easy, so start small. Start by blessing the one who harmed you. "Blessing" means to call upon God to give favor to another; it's something we do with our lips. When we bless with our lips first, it will become easier to follow through with kindness later.

PROVERBS 21:2

Every way of a man is right in his own eyes,
But the LORD weighs the hearts.

A t the Last Supper, Jesus announced that one of His closest companions—one of the Twelve—would betray Him. All of the disciples except Judas were perplexed and deeply troubled by this. They apparently began to examine their own hearts. Even Judas, ever careful to keep up the appearance of being like everyone else asked, "Rabbi, is it I?" But in his case there had been no sincere self-examination. He asked the question only because he was worried about how the others perceived him.

This event illustrates the degree to which Judas kept his public and private lives neatly divided. He had undoubtedly rationalized the plans he hatched in the private realm of his heart, yet he recognized that the public world he shared with Jesus and the other disciples would call his plans evil. The very fact that he had to keep his plans a secret should have been a clue that his mind was being deluded.

PSALM 119:11–12

Your word I have hidden in my heart,
That I might not sin against You.
Blessed are You, O LORD!
Teach me Your statutes.

The day of salvation closed for Judas. Divine mercy gave way to divine judgment, and Judas was handed over to Satan. But no one should be surprised, least of all Judas. He had developed the ability to keep his inner life from spilling over into his outward behavior, which is the last step before sin—usually on a grand scale—erupts into full, devastating expression. His divided life should have been a warning sign and his response to that warning could have made all the difference.

A double life is always a sign of impending disaster. James 1:8 says a double-minded man is unstable in all his ways. Judas epitomized that truth. His veneer of spiritual faithfulness was merely a disguise that could not last. The mask was about to come off, Judas's true character would be manifest, and Judas himself would be unable to live with the reality of what he really was.

JOHN 13:26–27

Jesus answered, "It is he to whom I shall give a piece of bread when I have dipped it." And having dipped the bread, He gave it to Judas Iscariot, the son of Simon. Now after the piece of bread, Satan entered him. Then Jesus said to him, "What you do, do quickly."

Jesus sent Judas away. He was not about to have the first communion service with the devil and Judas present in the room. Only after Judas had left did our Lord institute the Lord's Supper. And to this day, when we come to the Lord's Table, we are instructed to examine ourselves lest we come hypocritically to the table and bring judgment upon ourselves (1 Corinthians 11:27–32).

This is not because—as some suppose—some are unworthy of communion. None of us is worthy! Communion is not for sinless hearts; it is intended for contrite hearts. Communion is not for the sinless; it is intended for those who hate their sin. The Lord's Table is reserved for the Lord's people, those who have placed their trust in Christ to save them and to freely give them eternal life.

ROMANS 1:28

And even as they did not like to retain God in their knowledge, God gave them over to a debased mind, to do those things which are not fitting.

The apostle John says that throughout this entire episode, until Judas left the company of apostles, Jesus was deeply "troubled in spirit." Of course He was troubled! This wicked, wretched, Satan-possessed presence was polluting the fellowship of the apostles. Judas's ingratitude, his rejection of Jesus' kindness, the hate Judas secretly harbored for Jesus, the repulsiveness of the presence of Satan, the heinousness of sin, the horrors of knowing that the gaping jaws of hell were awaiting one of His closest companions—all of that troubled and agitated Jesus. No wonder He sent Judas away.

This is a dramatic illustration of how each individual who rejects Jesus in favor of his or her own sin will go into eternity. Judas—against every effort to dissuade him and in opposition to every divine kindness—chose his own fate, which Christ—with a heavy heart—sealed. Let it never be said that God condemned anyone who did not first condemn himself or herself.

Keep your heart with all diligence,
For out of it spring the issues of life.
Put away from you a deceitful mouth,
And put perverse lips far from you.

Remember, Judas did not act in a moment of insanity. This was not a sudden impulse. It was not an act borne only out of passion. This dark deed was deliberately planned and premeditated. He had been planning this for days, if not weeks or even months. He had already taken the money for it. He had just been waiting for the opportune hour. Then, Judas had nearly been unmasked by Jesus in front of the others. It was time for him to act.

The most destructive sins always begin "harmlessly" in the realm of imagination, and then fantasy. If tolerated there, they take firmer shape in the form of plans without intention, a harmless distraction to relieve conflict in the real world. But Satan—ever the enabler, ever the opportunist—will be certain to provide a means to turn imagined sin into full-blown, devastating reality.

Guard your heart!

MATTHEW 26:48–49

Now [Jesus'] betrayer had given [the soldiers] a sign, saying, "Whomever I kiss, He is the One; seize Him." Immediately he went up to Jesus and said, "Greetings, Rabbi!" and kissed Him.

The evening was at its end. Jesus had gone from the Upper Room to His customary place of prayer in the little olive grove known as Gethsemane. There He poured out his heart to the Father. Meanwhile, Judas led a cohort of Roman troops and a detachment of temple guards—perhaps as many as six hundred men—up to the garden under cover of night.

Judas identified Jesus with the greeting of a close friend, and he played the part with diabolical brilliance. The Greek term for "kiss" used by Matthew means "to kiss fervently." It's the same form used by Luke when describing the prodigal son's welcome. The word describes one falling on another with kisses, covering him with an enthusiastic shower of affection. Judas feigned love to the very end, perhaps thinking the others would not make the connection between Jesus' arrest and his involvement, thus continuing the charade. Secret sin had transformed Judas into a psychopath.

[A wealthy man said,] "I will say to my soul, 'Soul, you have many goods laid up for many years; take your ease; eat, drink, and be merry.'" But God said to him, "Fool! This night your soul will be required of you; then whose will those things be which you have provided?"

Judas sold Jesus for a pittance. This has to go down in history as the most incredibly stupid business transaction ever completed. Thirty silver coins was the traditional price of a slave and represented more than four months' wages for a typical worker. It was a significant sum, but nothing compared to the infinite worth of the Son of God! Judas traded a personal relationship with the Creator of the universe—who owns and commands everything in existence, and who promised to share everything with him—for the price of a common slave.

As stupid as that was, people make that same transaction every day. They worship provisions over the Provider; they treasure the gift rather than the Giver. And then they slip into eternity with no possessions, having traded their spiritual treasure for nothing.

What do you treasure above all else?

MATTHEW 27:3-4

Then Judas, His betrayer, seeing that He had been condemned, was remorseful and brought back the thirty pieces of silver to the chief priests and elders, saying, "I have sinned by betraying innocent blood." And they said, "What is that to us? You see to it!"

Judas's remorse was not the same as repentance, as subsequent events clearly show. He was sorry, not because he had sinned against Christ, but because his sin did not satisfy him the way he had hoped. That's the way sin always works. It always promises fulfillment, yet it always leaves the sinner emptier than before. This emptiness carried Judas into a hell of his own making. His conscience would not be silenced, and that is the very essence of hell. Sin brings guilt, and Judas's sin brought him unbearable misery. Again, his remorse was not genuine repentance. If that were the case, he would not have killed himself. He would have sought forgiveness.

As long as you have breath in your lungs, there is hope, even when engulfed in sin and smothered by remorse. Remorse is a good first step in the right direction, but it must be followed by repentance, a turning away from sin toward the Son of God.

When they had come to the place called Calvary, there they crucified Him,
and the criminals, one on the right hand and the other on the left. Then
Jesus said, "Father, forgive them, for they do not know what they do."

Judas did not seek the forgiveness of God. He did not cry out for mercy. He did not seek deliverance from Satan. Instead, he tried to silence his conscience by killing himself. He failed to acknowledge the message Christ had been preaching all along: nothing—not even death—can silence the condemning voice of sin except the voice of Christ on our behalf. He suffered the penalty of death for any who will turn from sin, and He offers eternal life for any who will receive His free gift of grace.

ROMANS 6:23

For the wages of sin is death, but the gift of God is eternal life in Christ Jesus our Lord.

The combined accounts of Matthew 27:6–8 and Acts 1:18–19 tell us that Judas hanged himself in a remote field and apparently hung unnoticed until his body decayed, fell onto some rocks below, and "burst open in the middle and all his entrails gushed out." This is virtually the last word in Scripture about Judas. His life and death were grotesque tragedies. And, ironically in the end, everything about Judas—inside and out—was exposed.

Sin cannot be hidden forever. It will eventually see the light of day. If it doesn't tragically spill out with devastating, destructive force in this life, it will certainly be exposed at the seat of God's judgment in the next. This truth presents us with a choice. We can bring our sin to God at the seat of judgment after death, or we can lay it down at the foot of the cross now.

MATTHEW 11:28–30

*[Jesus said,] "Come to Me, all you who labor and are heavy laden, and I
will give you rest. Take My yoke upon you and learn from Me, for I am
gentle and lowly in heart, and you will find rest for your souls. For My yoke
is easy and My burden is light."*

We can draw some important lessons from the life of Judas.
Judas is a tragic example of lost opportunity. He heard
Jesus teach day in and day out for two years or more. He could
have asked Jesus any question he liked. He could have sought
and received from the Lord any help he needed. He could have
exchanged the oppressive burden of his sin for an easy yoke. Yet
in the end Judas was damned because of his own failure to heed
what he heard.

How tragic for Judas. How tragic for us if we do not heed
his example and then heed the invitation of Christ to find rest
in Him.

JOHN 15:4−5

[Jesus said,] "Abide in Me, and I in you. As the branch cannot bear fruit of itself, unless it abides in the vine, neither can you, unless you abide in Me. I am the vine, you are the branches. He who abides in Me, and I in him, bears much fruit; for without Me you can do nothing."

Judas is also the epitome of wasted privilege. He was given the highest place of privilege among all the Lord's followers, but he squandered that privilege—cashed it in for a fistful of coins he decided he did not really want after all. What a stupid bargain!

As believers, we have unlimited access to the riches of God's grace, yet we choose to live in spiritual poverty, vainly seeking satisfaction in the world. Achievement, power, notoriety, sex, alcohol, career, relationships, possessions—all cheap substitutes for the abundant life promised to us by the Lord. We have been adopted as sons and we are heir to all that Christ commands, which is a place of privilege the Old Testament saints would have marveled at. To partake of His abundance, we need only remain close to Him. He has promised to take care of the rest.

2 CORINTHIANS 13:4−5

For though He was crucified in weakness, yet He lives by the power of God. For we also are weak in Him, but we shall live with Him by the power of God toward you. Examine yourselves as to whether you are in the faith. Test yourselves. Do you not know yourselves, that Jesus Christ is in you?—unless indeed you are disqualified.

Judas exemplifies the ugliness and danger of spiritual betrayal. Would that Judas were the only hypocrite who ever betrayed the Lord, but that is not so. There are Judases in every age—people who seem to be true disciples and close followers of Christ but who turn against Him for sinister and selfish reasons. Judas's life is a reminder to each of us about our need for self-examination.

While the Bible clearly teaches that a believer cannot lose his or her salvation, we all need periodic spiritual checkups. Scripture urges us to examine ourselves and test the reality of our faith in Christ every time we come to the Lord's table (1 Corinthians 11:28).

ROMANS 8:38–39

For I am persuaded that neither death nor life, nor angels nor principalities nor powers, nor things present nor things to come, nor height nor depth, nor any other created thing, shall be able to separate us from the love of God which is in Christ Jesus our Lord.

Judas is proof of the patient, forbearing goodness and loving-kindness of Christ. He even shows His love and grace to a reprobate like Judas. Remember, Jesus was still calling him "friend," even in the midst of Judas's betrayal. Jesus never showed the conniving disciple anything but kindness and charity, even though the Lord knew all along what Judas was planning to do. In no sense was Judas driven to do what he did by any mistreatment or provocation by Jesus.

This should give us overwhelming comfort as creatures who are notoriously fickle. A believer never need worry that his or her relationship with Christ is teetering on the brink of collapse and the next sin, however minor, just might push His patience beyond the limit. Nonsense! His love is not nearly as fragile as our resolve. In fact, nothing is greater than Christ's love for His own.

HEBREWS 2:14–15

Inasmuch then as the children have partaken of flesh and blood, He Himself likewise shared in the same, that through death He might destroy him who had the power of death, that is, the devil, and release those who through fear of death were all their lifetime subject to bondage.

The life of Judas demonstrates how the sovereign will of God cannot be thwarted by any means. His betrayal of Christ seemed at first glance like Satan's greatest triumph ever. But in reality, it signaled the utter defeat for the devil and all his works.

The same can be said of God's sovereign plan for each of His elect. Evil will seek to steal, kill, and destroy, and we will suffer the affliction of evil in the world, but we have God's promise that every circumstance will become His means of accomplishing the good He has foreordained for each of us. When darkness closes in around us, and evil appears to gain the upper hand, trust in the sovereignty and power and goodness of God is vital to maintaining hope.

LUKE 8:1–2

Now it came to pass, afterward, that He went through every city and village, preaching and bringing the glad tidings of the kingdom of God. And the twelve were with Him, and certain women who had been healed of evil spirits and infirmities—[including] Mary called Magdalene, out of whom had come seven demons.

Mary Magdalene is one of the best-known and least-understood names in Scripture. The Bible deliberately draws a curtain of silence over much of her life and personal background, but she still emerges as one of the prominent women of the New Testament. She has the eternal distinction of being the first person to whom Christ revealed Himself after the resurrection. This is made all the more significant by the fact that she had a very dark past as a woman Christ had liberated from demonic bondage.

Jesus said throughout His earthly ministry that He came to heal the sick and to redeem sinners. And no one represented the sick and sinful better than Mary Magdalene. In this way, she represents all of us. The God-man came to earth to liberate us from sin, He suffered the just penalty of sin on our behalf, He rose from the dead to give us new life, and He confronts us with His resurrection, to which we must—like Mary—respond in faith.

LUKE 9:42–43

As [the father of a demon-possessed boy] was still coming, the demon threw him down and convulsed him. Then Jesus rebuked the unclean spirit, healed the child, and gave him back to his father. And they were all amazed at the majesty of God.

I n every case, demon possession is portrayed in Scripture as an affliction, not a sin, per se. Lawlessness, superstition, and idolatry undoubtedly have a major role in opening a person's heart to demonic possession, but none of the demonized individuals in the New Testament is explicitly associated with immoral behavior. Scripture deliberately and mercifully omits the macabre details of Mary's dreadful demon possession. Unfortunately, many over the centuries have been all too willing to fill in the details with the product of their own twisted imaginations.

Regardless, the fact remains that Mary Magdalene's sin—whatever it was—is no business of ours. What's important is that she was forgiven and healed, just like each one of us. And, just like us, she was made extraordinary by the amazing grace of God through His Son.

LUKE 8:1–3

The twelve were with Him, and certain women who had been healed of evil spirits and infirmities—Mary called Magdalene, out of whom had come seven demons, and Joanna the wife of Chuza, Herod's steward, and Susanna, and many others who provided for Him from their substance.

Mary Magdalene joined the close circle of disciples who traveled with Jesus on His long journeys. Luke included her with the other women who provided for Jesus and the disciples from her substance (Luke 8:3). Perhaps she had inherited financial resources that she used for the support of Jesus and His disciples. The fact that her name appears at the head of the list of his band of women seems to indicate that she had a special place of respect among them.

It is true that most rabbis in Jesus' time did not normally call women to become their disciples. But Christ encouraged men and women alike to take His yoke and learn from Him. This is yet another evidence of how women are honored in Scripture. It is also a testament to the value of women in Christ's kingdom. In fact, wherever Christianity goes in the world, the status of women improves dramatically in that culture.

MATTHEW 27:55–56

Many women who followed Jesus from Galilee, ministering to Him, were there looking on from afar, among whom were Mary Magdalene, Mary the mother of James and Joses, and the mother of Zebedee's sons.

When the other disciples forsook Jesus, Mary Magdalene remained His faithful disciple. In fact, she first appeared in Luke's gospel at a time when opposition to Jesus had grown to the point that He began to teach in parables. When others became offended with His sayings, she stayed by His side. She followed Him all the way from Galilee to Jerusalem for that final Passover celebration, through the trials, to the cross, and then beyond. She remained longer than any other disciple at the cross, and she was the first to reach His tomb at daybreak on the first day of the week.

The most important quality of a genuine disciple is devotion. True disciples stay close to their masters. Mary's devotion foreshadowed that of the martyrs, whose courage allowed them to proclaim the good news of their Master, even at the cost of their own lives.

Are you a disciple?

JOHN 20:16–17

Jesus said to her, "Mary!" She turned and said to Him, "Rabboni!" (which is to say, Teacher). Jesus said to her, "Do not cling to Me, for I have not yet ascended to My Father; but go to My brethren and say to them, 'I am ascending to My Father and your Father, and to My God and your God.'"

At first, Mary was devastated by the thought that someone had stolen the body of Jesus, so when He appeared to her, Mary's grief instantly turned to inexpressible joy. She appears to have embraced Him as if she would never let Him go. Most of us are too much like Thomas—hesitant, pessimistic. Mary, by contrast, didn't want to release Him.

Jesus thus conferred on her a unique and unparalleled honor, allowing her to be the first to see and hear Him after His resurrection. Others had already heard and believed the glad news from the mouth of an angel. Mary got to hear it first from Jesus Himself. That was her extraordinary legacy. No one can ever share that honor or take it from her. But we can, and should, seek to imitate her deep love for Christ.

Ecclesiastes 7:3

Sorrow is better than laughter,
For by a sad countenance the heart is made better.

Most people know Thomas by his nickname, "Doubting Thomas," but that may not be the most fitting label for him. He was a better man than the popular lore would indicate. It is probably fair, however, to say that Thomas was a somewhat negative person—a worrywart, a brooder, anxious, and angst-ridden. He anticipated the worst and remained skeptical of good news.

Melancholy personalities tend to make people feel uneasy. We prefer our leaders to be positive, even bubbly in the face of challenges. So we would probably find Thomas unpleasant to be around and perhaps even lacking in faith. However, many of our most extraordinary leaders—like Abraham Lincoln, C. H. Spurgeon, and Winston Churchill—were more like brooding Thomas than irrepressible Peter.

Whatever your temperament, Christ didn't call you to follow Him because of your personality. You are His disciple because He loves you. While the Holy Spirit will transform your heart, He does not expect you to become someone else. The "you" God made is the person He desires, and He wants to give you as a gift to others.

Then Jesus said to them plainly, "Lazarus is dead. And I am glad for your sakes that I was not there, that you may believe. Nevertheless let us go to him." Then Thomas, who is called the Twin, said to his fellow disciples, "Let us also go, that we may die with Him."

It becomes obvious from John's gospel that Thomas had a tendency to look only into the darkest corners of life. He seemed always to anticipate the worst of everything. Yet despite his pessimism, some wonderfully redeeming elements of his character come through.

Jesus had left Jerusalem because His life was in jeopardy there, and He taught multitudes in the rough country where John the Baptist once taught. But something happened to interrupt their time in the seclusion and safety of the wilderness. His friend, Lazarus, had fallen gravely ill. Everyone knew that visiting him would place Jesus dangerously close to the murderous clutches of His enemies. Nevertheless, Thomas rallied the other disciples, saying, "Let us also go, that we may die with Him."

Not exactly an optimistic outlook, but certainly reasonable. Take note of his courage. I'll take a loyal pessimist over a fickle optimist any day.

PHILIPPIANS 1:27–28

*Only let your conduct be worthy of the gospel of Christ, so that whether I
come and see you or am absent, I may hear of your affairs, that you stand
fast in one spirit, with one mind striving together for the faith of the gospel,
and not in any way terrified by your adversaries, which is to them a proof of
perdition, but to you of salvation, and that from God.*

It's not easy to be a pessimist. It is a miserable way to live. An
optimist might have said, "Let's go; everything will work out.
The Lord knows what He's doing. He says we won't stumble. We'll
be fine." But the pessimist says, "He's going to die, and we're going
to die with Him." Thomas at least had the courage to remain loyal,
even in the face of his pessimism. It is much easier for an optimist
to be loyal. He always expects the best. Therefore, I admire Thomas's
heroic pessimism. This was genuine devotion to Christ, even if his
perspective was tainted with gloom.

The fact of the matter is, the outlook for Christ's followers is
not always rosy. Jesus promised hatred and persecution from the
world, which "hated Me before it hated you" (John 15:18). So
when the going gets tough, where will you be?

ROMANS 6:4-5

We were buried with Him through baptism into death, that just as Christ was raised from the dead by the glory of the Father, even so we also should walk in newness of life. For if we have been united together in the likeness of His death, certainly we also shall be in the likeness of His resurrection.

Thomas was devoted to Christ. He may have been the equal to John in this regard. It is clear from this account that Thomas did not want to live without Jesus. If his Master was going to die, Thomas was prepared to die with Him. In essence, he says, "Guys, suck it up; let's go and die. Better to die and be with Christ than to be left behind."

We should not see this as fatalism; it's not that Thomas didn't care about living or dying. On the contrary, he wanted to live very much. However, he also recognized that life apart from God is no life at all. And in this respect Thomas saw things clearly. His future was inextricably bound to Christ's. Fortunately, the same is true for all who are in Christ.

JOHN 11:14–16

Then Jesus said to them plainly, "Lazarus is dead. And I am glad for your sakes that I was not there, that you may believe. Nevertheless let us go to him." Then Thomas, who is called the Twin, said to his fellow disciples, "Let us also go, that we may die with Him."

Thomas was an example of strength to the rest of the apostles. His deep devotion to Christ could not be dampened even by his own pessimism and he followed Jesus with undaunted courage, which was undoubtedly inspiring. It appears the others collectively followed his lead at this point and said, "Okay, let's go and die"— because they *did* go with Him to Bethany.

Sometimes we need someone to step to the fore when the collective courage of a group is needed. And the valor of a pessimist is always more inspiring than the rally cry of a Pollyanna.

What challenges do you currently face? Are you prepared to count the cost and be an example of strength for others?

[Jesus said,] "I am the vine, you are the branches. He who abides in Me, and I in him, bears much fruit; for without Me you can do nothing."

Thomas's profound love for the Lord shows up again during the disciples' last supper with their Master before His crucifixion. Jesus said, "I go to prepare a place for you . . . and where I go you know, and the way you know" (John 14:2, 4). But Thomas replied, "Lord, we do not know where You are going, and how can we know the way?" (v. 5). Again we see his pessimism. In essence, he was saying, "You're leaving. It was a better plan for us to die with You, because then there's no separation. If we died together, we would all be together."

Here is a man with a strong connection with his Lord and the thought of losing Christ paralyzed him. While his connection with the Lord was more tangible, ours is no less vital. Yet—let's be honest—we don't treat it as such. If we don't neglect relationships we genuinely value, why would we fail to invest in our bond with Christ?

ROMANS 12:15

Rejoice with those who rejoice, and weep with those who weep.

The thought of living without Christ was overwhelming for Thomas. And his worst fears came to pass. Jesus died and he didn't. Later, when the other disciples got together to comfort one another, Thomas was not with them (John 20:24). It is too bad he wasn't there. Jesus came and appeared to them, but Thomas missed the whole event. Why wasn't he with them? It's possible he was so negative, so pessimistic, such a melancholy person, that he was off somewhere alone, wallowing in his misery.

We need one another when recovering from a great loss, such as the death of someone close. While some solitude is necessary during times of grief, it can be deadly in large doses. God gave us one another to share burdens. Moreover, we might also forfeit something even more wonderful by shunning company in our sorrow.

JOHN 20:25

The other disciples therefore said to him, "We have seen the Lord." So he said to them, "Unless I see in His hands the print of the nails, and put my finger into the print of the nails, and put my hand into His side, I will not believe."

Thomas may well have felt alone, betrayed, rejected, forsaken. It was over. The One he loved so deeply was gone, and it tore his heart out. When he eventually saw his friends, they said, "We have seen the Lord!" They were exuberant, eager to share the news with Thomas. But he was still being a hopeless pessimist. The news was too good to be true. Then he uttered the words that would forever label him "the doubter."

Don't be too hard on Thomas. Remember, the other disciples didn't believe in the resurrection until they saw Jesus, either. What set Thomas apart from the other ten was not that his doubt was greater, but that his sorrow was greater. And sorrow has a way of dousing the bright of day with the gloom of night.

Note that no one derided Thomas. Rather than condemning his doubt, they empathized with his sorrow. Furthermore, they trusted that the Lord would care for Thomas in His time, in His way.

1 THESSALONIANS 4:13–14

But I do not want you to be ignorant, brethren, concerning those who have fallen asleep, lest you sorrow as others who have no hope. For if we believe that Jesus died and rose again, even so God will bring with Him those who sleep in Jesus.

Eight days passed after Jesus appeared to the disciples again. Finally, Thomas's ragged grief apparently had eased a bit. Because when the apostles returned to the room where Jesus appeared earlier, Thomas joined them. Once again the Lord came to them, saying "Peace to you!"

Each person experiences grief and sorrow differently. Therefore, each must be allowed to process the pain of loss in his or her own way, taking the time he or she needs. And unless the behavior becomes disturbing or destructive, the grief-stricken should be encouraged to do whatever is necessary to heal. While excessive gloom is a normal stage of grief, it must, nevertheless, give way to hope. Death is not the end for the believer. We do not grieve as those who are not in Christ. The resurrection allows us to anticipate life after death—our own and of those we treasure.

Then [Jesus] said to Thomas, "Reach your finger here, and look at My hands; and reach your hand here, and put it into My side. Do not be unbelieving, but believing."

No one needed to tell Jesus what Thomas had said, of course. At this next appearance, He immediately addressed Thomas, gently and compassionately. Thomas had erred because he was more or less wired to be a pessimist. But it was the error of a profound love. It was provoked by grief, brokenheartedness, uncertainty, and the pain of loneliness. No one could feel the way Thomas felt unless he loved Jesus the way Thomas loved Him.

Identifying with Thomas's gloom should lead us to acknowledge and admire his heroic devotion to Christ, which made him understand that it would be better to die than to be separated from his Lord. If only we loved Christ that much! Moreover, the darkest gloom at the thought of losing Him should turn to the brightest hope with the knowledge that those in Christ will never be without their Lord! No loss we ever face can overshadow the joy of that truth. Therefore, do not be unbelieving, but believing.

For we do not have a High Priest who cannot sympathize with our
weaknesses, but was in all points tempted as we are, yet without sin.

The Lord was amazingly gentle with Thomas, for he erred honestly—as a result of his profoundly deep love for his Master. Jesus understands our weaknesses. So He understands our doubt. He sympathizes with our uncertainty. He is patient with our pessimism. However, He will not leave us to struggle on our own. He intercedes on our behalf as our great High Priest, and He faithfully confronts us with truth.

When the time was right and Thomas's heart was ready, Jesus confronted him with the truth of His resurrection. Then Thomas made what was probably the greatest statement ever to come from the lips of Jesus' apostles: "My Lord and my God!" (John 20:28). Let those who question the deity of Christ meet Thomas.

ACTS 1:8

[Jesus said,] "You shall receive power when the Holy Spirit has come upon you; and you shall be witnesses to Me in Jerusalem, and in all Judea and Samaria, and to the end of the earth."

After encountering his risen Lord, suddenly Thomas's melancholy, comfortless, negative, moody tendencies were forever banished. And in that moment he was transformed into a great evangelist. A short time later, at Pentecost, along with the other apostles, he was filled with the Holy Spirit and empowered for ministry. He, like his comrades, took the gospel to the ends of the earth.

A considerable amount of ancient testimony suggests Thomas carried the gospel as far as India. There is to this day a small hill near the airport in Chennai (Madras), India, where Thomas is believed to have been buried. There are churches in south India whose roots are traceable to the beginning of the church age, and tradition says they were founded under the ministry of Thomas. The strongest traditions say he was martyred for his faith by being run through by a spear—a fitting form of martyrdom for one whose faith came of age when he saw the spear mark in his Master's side and for one who longed to be reunited with his Lord.

JOHN 20:28

Jesus said to him, "Thomas, because you have seen Me, you have believed. Blessed are those who have not seen and yet have believed."

It's interesting that God used a publican like Matthew and a pessimist like Thomas. Matthew was once the vilest of sinners—a wretched, despicable outcast. Thomas was a tenderhearted, moody, melancholy individual. But both of them were transformed by Christ in the same way He transformed others.

Are you beginning to get the idea of what kind of people God wants? He wants everyone and can use *anyone*. Personality, status, and family background are all immaterial. The one thing all these men except Judas had in common was a willingness to acknowledge their own sinfulness and look to Christ for grace. He met them with grace, mercy, and forgiveness and transformed their lives into lives that would glorify Him.

Where do you stand? Have you come to Christ acknowledging your sinfulness, seeking His grace? That is the essence of belief. And when you believe in Him, He will meet you with grace, mercy, and forgiveness and then begin the amazing work of transformation.

One of the two who heard John speak, and followed Jesus, was Andrew, Simon Peter's brother. He first found his own brother Simon, and said to him, "We have found the Messiah" (which is translated, the Christ). And he brought him to Jesus.

Peter's brother, Andrew, is the least-known of the four disciples in the lead group, and he was not included in several of the important events where we see Peter, James, and John together with Christ. However, there is no question that he had a particularly close relationship with Jesus because he was so often the means by which other people were personally introduced to the Master. He was the first to be called, he was responsible for introducing Peter to Christ, he brought the young boy to Jesus at the feeding of the five thousand, and he led God-fearing Greeks to meet the Jewish Messiah after His triumphal entry.

Not all disciples need to be in the center of the action to be effective in the cause of Christ. Some prefer to dwell on the outskirts of Christianity, where they have greater opportunity to encounter outsiders and invite them in. How marvelous that God would balance Peter-like disciples with people of quiet influence, like Andrew.

MATTHEW 6:1

"Take heed that you do not do your charitable deeds before men, to be seen by them. Otherwise you have no reward from your Father in heaven."

Andrew and his brother, Peter, had probably been lifelong companions with the other set of fishermen—brothers from Capernaum—James and John, sons of Zebedee. So it was quite natural that this little group formed a cohesive unit within the Twelve. Of the four disciples in the inner circle, Andrew was the least conspicuous, living mostly in the shadow of his better-known brother. However, there is no evidence that he begrudged Peter's dominance. Almost everything Scripture tells us about Andrew shows that he had the right heart for effective ministry in the background. He was evidently pleased to do what he could with the gifts and calling God had bestowed on him, and he allowed the others to do likewise.

How we need men and women like Andrew in our churches! In fact, our more forceful, natural leaders could stand to learn from Andrew's example. He is a wonderful illustration of how someone can positively impact the people of God with quiet, unassuming strength.

LUKE 22:25–26

And He said to them, "The kings of the Gentiles exercise lordship over them, and those who exercise authority over them are called 'benefactors.' But not so among you; on the contrary, he who is greatest among you, let him be as the younger, and he who governs as he who serves."

Of all the disciples in the inner circle, Andrew appears the least contentious and the most thoughtful. Interestingly, his name means "manly." Peter was brash, hasty, impulsive, and domineering. James and John were nicknamed "Sons of Thunder" because of their hotheaded and reckless tendencies. They were evidently the ones who provoked many of the arguments about who was the greatest. But there's never a hint of that with Andrew. When he speaks—which is rare in Scripture—he always says the right thing. Whenever he acts apart from the other disciples, he does what is right. (Did I mention that his name means "manly"?)

Andrew proves that the best kind of strength is tender, unassuming, practical, and always helpful. Look around your organizations. See if you can identify the "Andrews" quietly moving things along in the right direction. They aren't hard to find if you take time to look. Then find a way to thank and encourage them.

JOHN 5:44

"How can you believe, who receive honor from one another, and do not seek the honor that comes from the only God?"

A ndrew and Peter, though brothers, had totally different leadership styles. But just as Peter was perfectly suited for his calling, Andrew was perfectly suited for his. In fact, Andrew may be a better model for most church leaders than Peter, because most who enter the ministry will labor in relative obscurity, like Andrew, as opposed to being renowned and prominent, like Peter.

Beware those who enter the ministry for the sake of fame, fortune, and glory. Those who crave the limelight cannot be the kind of servant-leaders Christ calls us to be. God may sometimes elevate a man to a position of great influence, but the only proper motive for ministry is the glory and preeminence of Christ alone (Colossians 1:18). Those who seek prominence for themselves are actually detrimental to the work of Christ (Philippians 2:3; 3 John 9).

MATTHEW 5:5-6

Blessed are the meek,
For they shall inherit the earth.
Blessed are those who hunger and thirst for righteousness,
For they shall be filled.

Andrew's name means "manly," and it seems a fitting description. Of course, the kind of net fishing he and the others did required no small degree of physical strength and machismo. But Andrew also had other characteristics of manliness. He was bold, decisive, and deliberate. Nothing about him was feeble or wimpish. He was driven by a hearty passion for the truth, and he was willing to subject himself to the most extreme kinds of hardship and austerity in pursuit of that objective. We know that because, before following Christ, he was a disciple of John the Baptist, well-known for his wilderness living, camel's hair garment, and diet of locusts and wild honey. To follow John, one could hardly be soft.

Our culture tends to think of meek people as mousy or sheepish, but nothing could be further from the truth. Meek people are the finest examples of strength and determination; doers, not talkers. These people simply do what must be done, no matter how hard, and then allow the results of their deeds speak for themselves.

JOHN 1:35–37

John stood with two of his disciples. And looking at Jesus as He walked, he said, "Behold the Lamb of God!" The two disciples heard him speak, and they followed Jesus.

When John the Baptist proved to be a genuine prophet—the first in more than four hundred years—Andrew moved to the desert. And for months he listened as the Baptizer proclaimed the coming of Messiah. So, when Jesus walked by and John exclaimed, "Behold, the Lamb of God!" (John 1:36), Andrew was understandably excited and wasted no time. He and his fishing partner from Capernaum followed Jesus home. Andrew didn't seek attention, but he definitely wanted to be where the action was.

Leaders desperately want Andrews on their teams. They need behind-the-scenes people who want to be involved and want to put their effort where it will make the most difference. Unfortunately, most people who volunteer for those positions also want to be noticed. If you're an Andrew, you are a rare and precious commodity.

JOHN 1:40–42

One of the two who heard John speak, and followed Him, was Andrew, Simon Peter's brother. He first found his own brother Simon, and said to him, "We have found the Messiah" (which is translated, the Christ). And he brought him to Jesus.

A ndrew and John spent the afternoon and evening in private fellowship with Jesus, and they left convinced that they had found the true Messiah. When they left, Andrew immediately went and found the one person in the world whom he most loved—whom he most wanted to know Jesus—and he led him to Christ.

Of course, Andrew would have been fully aware of Peter's tendency to domineer. He must have known full well that as soon as Peter entered the company of disciples, he would take charge and Andrew would be relegated to a secondary status. Yet Andrew brought his brother anyway. That fact alone says much about his character.

Strong people are rarely threatened by natural leadership or even gregarious personalities. They care most about doing what's right, no matter who receives the credit or gains attention. As you examine your motives, what do you care most about? Can you find satisfaction in positively impacting the world around you if no one ever discovers your contribution?

MATTHEW 18:5–6

"Whoever receives one little child like this in My name receives Me.
Whoever causes one of these little ones who believe in Me to sin, it would be
better for him if a millstone were hung around his neck, and he were
drowned in the depth of the sea."

Andrew's willingness to stand in the background often gave him a unique perspective. He frequently gained insights into things the other disciples had trouble grasping. Thus, whenever he does come to the forefront, one cannot help but notice his uncanny ability to see immense value in small and modest things. For example, Andrew fully appreciated the value of a single soul. He was known for bringing individuals, not crowds, to Jesus.

Ministries can sometimes become distracted by programs, buildings, numbers, and community impact. But we must never overlook the true reason ministries exist: individuals in relationship with Jesus Christ. Andrew-like disciples bring us all back to reality because they never allow anything to distract them from the needs of individuals.

JOHN 12:20–22

Now there were certain Greeks among those who came up to worship at the feast. Then they came to Philip, who was from Bethsaida of Galilee, and asked him, saying, "Sir, we wish to see Jesus." Philip came and told Andrew, and in turn Andrew and Philip told Jesus.

Jesus' triumphal entry into Jerusalem caught the attention of some God-fearing Gentiles. The men approached Philip and said, "Sir, we wish to see Jesus" (John 12:21). It is significant that these men came to Philip, but Philip took the men to Andrew. Why? We can only conjecture. Nevertheless, he knew Andrew would take action and get them to Christ. And apparently Andrew was very comfortable in this role.

One thing I have observed in all my years of ministry is that the most effective and important aspects of evangelism usually take place on an individual, personal level. Most people do not come to Christ as an immediate response to a sermon they hear in a crowded setting. They come to Christ because of the influence of an individual.

Keep that in mind, and allow both your life and your lips to give testimony to your neighbors and loved ones about Christ. The circle of your immediate relationships is the first and most important arena for you to be a herald of the gospel.

1 PETER 3:15

Sanctify the Lord God in your hearts, and always be ready to give a defense to everyone who asks you a reason for the hope that is in you, with meekness and fear.

Both Andrew and Peter had evangelistic hearts, but their methods were radically different. Peter preached at Pentecost, and three thousand people were added to the church. Nothing in Scripture indicates that Andrew ever preached to a crowd or stirred masses of people. But don't think that his impact wasn't enormous. It was. Remember that it was he who brought Peter to Christ. All the fruit of Peter's ministry is ultimately the fruit of Andrew's faithful, individual witness.

God often works that way. He may not have called you to proclaim the good news of Jesus Christ to stadiums full of people. But within your sphere of influence are many who need the gospel, and God is preparing hearts to hear the gospel from you. Don't underestimate what God can do through your faithful testimony.

COLOSSIANS 4:5-6

Walk in wisdom toward those who are outside, redeeming the time. Let your speech always be with grace, seasoned with salt, that you may know how you ought to answer each one.

A ndrew was not confused when someone wanted to see Jesus. He simply brought them to Him. He understood that Jesus would want to meet anyone who wanted to meet Him.

That's the way Andrew usually ministered: one-on-one. Most pastors would love to have their churches populated by people with Andrew's mentality. Too many Christians think that because they can't speak in front of groups or because they don't have leadership gifts, they aren't responsible to evangelize. There are a few who, like Andrew, understand the value of befriending just one person and bringing him or her to Christ.

Evangelizing isn't as hard as most people fear it to be. They worry about fumbling their words or forcing the issue. If you are a believer, most conversations will naturally take a spiritual turn without your trying. Focus on the need of the person, not what you feel obligated to say, and before you know it, you'll be walking toward Christ with your friend in tow.

JOHN 6:8–10

One of His disciples, Andrew, Simon Peter's brother, said to Him, "There is a lad here who has five barley loaves and two small fish, but what are they among so many?" Then Jesus said, "Make the people sit down."

Some people see the big picture more clearly just because they appreciate the value of small things. Andrew fit that category. When five thousand men and their families needed feeding in the wilderness, Jesus gave His disciples the task of coming up with a plan. Philip did a quick accounting and determined that they had neither the money to buy enough food nor the time to locate it. At that point, Andrew spoke up. "There is a lad here who has five barley loaves and two small fish" (John 6:9).

Now, Andrew was no fool. He knew that the little boy's lunch basket was not enough by itself. But he also knew the Lord would not issue a command without making it possible to obey. So he identified the one food source available and made sure Jesus knew about it. Something in him seemed to understand that no gift is insignificant in the hands of Jesus.

What you have may not seem like much to you, but in the hands of Jesus it's an abundance.

JOHN 6:11–13

And Jesus took the loaves, and when He had given thanks He distributed them to the disciples, and the disciples to those sitting down; and likewise of the fish, as much as they wanted. So when they were filled, He said to His disciples, "Gather up the fragments that remain, so that nothing is lost." Therefore they gathered them up, and filled twelve baskets with the fragments of the five barley loaves which were left over by those who had eaten.

Jesus taught His disciples on more than one occasion that the true measure of a gift's significance is the sacrificial faithfulness of the giver, not the size of the gift. That's a difficult concept for the human mind, but somehow Andrew seemed instinctively to know that he was not wasting Jesus' time by bringing such a paltry amount of food. His belief in his Master set the stage for a miracle.

It is not the greatness of the gift that impacts the world, but rather the greatness of the God to whom it is given. Don't hold back. Give what you have to the Lord, paltry as it may be. Then let Him astound you with what He is able to do with it.

ACTS 17:24–25

God, who made the world and everything in it, since He is Lord of heaven and earth, does not dwell in temples made with hands. Nor is He worshiped with men's hands, as though He needed anything, since He gives to all life, breath, and all things.

Jesus didn't need anything to feed the multitude in the wilderness, least of all a little boy's lunch basket. He could have materialized bread and fish—or anything else, for that matter—from thin air. But the way He fed the five thousand illustrates the way God prefers to work. He takes the sacrificial and often insignificant gifts of people who give faithfully, and He multiplies them to accomplish monumental things.

As the Lord has formulated His plan, we take care of the addition, He will be responsible for the multiplication, and together we share the victory—not because He needs us, but because He loves us.

MATTHEW 6:2–4

"Therefore, when you do a charitable deed, do not sound a trumpet before you as the hypocrites do in the synagogues and in the streets, that they may have glory from men. Assuredly, I say to you, they have their reward. But when you do a charitable deed, do not let your left hand know what your right hand is doing, that your charitable deed may be in secret; and your Father who sees in secret will Himself reward you openly."

It takes a special kind of person to be a leader with a servant's heart. Andrew was like that. As far as we know, he never preached to multitudes or founded any churches. He never wrote an epistle. He isn't mentioned in the book of Acts or any of the epistles. Andrew is more a silhouette than a portrait in the pages of Scripture, much like he was in life. In fact, the Bible does not record what happened to Andrew after Pentecost. Whatever role he played in the early church, he remained behind the scenes.

We would be wrong to think his impact was small, however. Because he chose to live quietly and serve inconspicuously, we will see little direct evidence of his contributions. But rest assured, heaven knows and the Father has assuredly greeted him with a warm, "Well done."

Consider how you might subtly yet profoundly impact the people around you for the sake of Christ. Think like Andrew: one person at a time.

1 CORINTHIANS 1:27–29

But God has chosen the foolish things of the world to put to shame the wise, and God has chosen the weak things of the world to put to shame the things which are mighty; and the base things of the world and the things which are despised God has chosen, and the things which are not, to bring to nothing the things that are, that no flesh should glory in His presence.

Andrew's legacy is the example he left to show us that in effective ministry it is often the little things that count—the individual people, the insignificant gifts, and the inconspicuous service. God delights to use such things. He delights to bring ordinary people close to himself, to transform them from the inside out, and then do extraordinary things through them. More often than not, those extraordinary deeds are known only to Him. But then, His approval is all that really counts, right?

HOSEA 14:9

Who is wise?
Let him understand these things.
Who is prudent?
Let him know them.
For the ways of the Lord are right;
The righteous walk in them,
But transgressors stumble in them.

From the time she became Abraham's wife, Sarah desired one thing above all others, and that was to have children. But she was barren throughout her normal childbearing years and tortured by her childlessness. Every recorded episode of ill temper or strife in her household was related to this frustration. It ate at her. She spent years in the grip of frustration and depression because of it. She finally concluded that God Himself was restraining her from having children.

Indeed, He was—but not as chastisement against Sarah. Her barrenness was in no way an expression of His displeasure. But His plan for her was even better than what she longed for, and His timing, as always, was perfect.

Sometimes God's greatest blessings come to us disguised as trials. The best way to endure those trials is to remember that God is sovereign, His plan for us is good, and He is always right in *all* His ways.

GENESIS 16:2

So Sarai said to Abram, "See now, the LORD has restrained me from bearing children. Please, go in to my maid; perhaps I shall obtain children by her." And Abram heeded the voice of Sarai.

Abraham and Sarah were perplexed by her barrenness. The Lord had promised that Abraham would be the patriarch of a nation of covenant people. So, Sarah—perhaps thinking that God needed help with His plan—concocted a scheme that was immoral, unrighteous, and utterly foolish. She rashly persuaded Abraham to father a child by her own handmaid. Predictably, the consequences of such a carnal ploy nearly tore her life apart and seemed to leave a lasting scar on her personality. She eventually insisted that Abraham throw the other woman out, along with the child he had fathered by her.

This should go without saying, but God does not need help accomplishing His will. Beware the temptation to advance God's plan *your* way, according to *your* schedule, especially if an action involves sin. Suddenly, everything that should be right will be all wrong.

By faith Sarah herself also received strength to conceive seed, and she bore a child when she was past the age, because she judged Him faithful who had promised.

Sarah's faults are obvious enough. She was certainly fallen. Her faith, at times, grew weak. Her own heart sometimes led her astray. Those shortcomings were conspicuous and undeniable. If those things were all we knew about Sarah, we might be tempted to picture her as something of a battle-ax—a harsh, severe woman, relentlessly self-centered, and temperamental. She wasn't always the kind of person who naturally evokes our sympathy and understanding.

Fortunately, there was much more to Sarah than that. She had important strengths as well. Like many people, Sarah was a tender soul wrapped in a beautiful yet steely exterior. Take the time to get beyond her initial severity and you discover a woman characterized by humility, meekness, hospitality, faithfulness, deep affection for her husband, sincere love toward God, and hope that never died.

She's a reminder that we should not judge others quickly or too harshly. "Do not judge according to appearance, but judge with righteous judgment" (John 7:24).

GENESIS 18:10–12

[The angel] said, "I will certainly return to you according to the time of life, and behold, Sarah your wife shall have a son." (Sarah was listening in the tent door which was behind him.) Now Abraham and Sarah were old, well advanced in age; and Sarah had passed the age of childbearing. Therefore Sarah laughed within herself, saying, "After I have grown old, shall I have pleasure, my lord being old also?"

Sarah obviously had a key role to play in God's plan to establish His covenant with a new race of people. Abraham could never become the patriarch of the Hebrew nation if she did not first become mother to his offspring. She was surely aware of the Lord's promises to Abraham. She certainly would have longed to see those promises fulfilled. As long as she remained childless, however, the sense that everything somehow hinged on her must have pressed on her like a great burden on her shoulders.

Perhaps you, too, find yourself at the focal point of God's plan in some way. If you are a leader or teacher, if you're a mother or father of young people looking to you for spiritual guidance, if you are a solitary Christian where you work—the responsibility can feel overwhelming. Take heart. God doesn't expect you to do the heavy lifting in accomplishing His plan. He will see to its success. Your responsibility is to faithfully trust Him.

[God said to Abraham,] "I will make you a great nation; I will bless you and make your name great; and you shall be a blessing. I will bless those who bless you, and I will curse him who curses you; and in you all the families of the earth shall be blessed."

What energized Sarah's willingness to leave all familiar surroundings, sever ties with her family, and commit to a life of rootless wandering? God's promise. It was unconditional and literally unlimited in the scope of its blessings. The promised blessing even had eternal implications. In other words, redemption from sin and the means of salvation from divine judgment were part and parcel of the promise (Galatians 3:8, 16–17). Sarah understood that promise. According to Scripture, she believed it.

The very nature of trust in God involves earthly inconvenience, mitigated by the promise of eternal blessing. That's because this world has been twisted by sin after the Fall and remains fundamentally opposed to its Creator and His ways. Don't expect life to be easy when you place your faith in Christ. In many respects, life will be more difficult. However, you will not be left alone, and the blessings far outweigh the trials.

Then God said to Abraham, "As for Sarai your wife, you shall not call her name Sarai, but Sarah shall be her name. And I will bless her and also give you a son by her; then I will bless her, and she shall be a mother of nations; kings of peoples shall be from her."

By the time Abraham and Sarah began their journey in obedience to God's instructions, Sarah was sixty-five, which was by no means young, even by the standards of the patriarchal era. The life of a nomad would be hard for anyone at sixty-five. And yet there is no sign whatsoever that she was reluctant or unwilling to go with Abraham to a land neither of them had ever seen. In fact, Sarah evidently went eagerly, gladly, and enthusiastically.

Her willingness to follow Abraham where the Lord led him was an expression of her own personal faith. Knowing that her husband was following the clear call of the Lord, she encouraged and supported his journey of faith. Their life together was an adventure. Though it was not always easy, they walked together and trusted God together, knowing that in the end the reward of their faith would make all their trials seem paltry. That is the very essence of true faith (Hebrews 11:8–19).

GENESIS 12:12-13

[Abraham said,] "Therefore it will happen, when the Egyptians see you, that they will say, 'This is his wife'; and they will kill me, but they will let you live. Please say you are my sister, that it may be well with me for your sake, and that I may live because of you."

After Abraham and Sarah settled in Canaan, a severe famine led them to Egypt for provisions. It was there, for the first time, that Abraham tried to pass Sarah off as his sister, out of fear that Pharaoh might kill him and take Sarah into his harem. (Of course, this was a half-truth, because Sarah was Abraham's half sister). The patriarch's motives were selfish and cowardly, and the scheme reflected a serious weakness in his faith. But Sarah's devotion to her husband is nonetheless commendable—while undoubtedly painful to bear—and God honored her for it.

This illustrates how devotion to the husband and submission to his leadership sometimes come at great personal cost to the wife—which is what makes deferring to a husband's decisions a serious matter of faith. It also illustrates why every husband must take his leadership role very seriously. A husband's obedience to God is always in the best interests of the wife—and a husband's disobedience can put his wife directly in harm's way. In this case, Abraham's choice to hide behind a lie not only dishonored God; it also put Sarah in grave spiritual and physical danger.

GENESIS 12:15–16

*The princes of Pharaoh also saw [Sarah] and commended her to Pharaoh.
And the woman was taken to Pharaoh's house. He treated Abram well for
her sake. He had sheep, oxen, male donkeys, male and female servants,
female donkeys, and camels.*

Eventually, Pharaoh discovered that recent plagues on his house
were caused by Sarah's presence in his harem (although he had
not yet violated her). After confronting Abraham with the deception, he expelled the patriarch and his wife from Egypt. Nonetheless,
Pharaoh, preoccupied with more pressing things, did no harm to
either of them, and when they left, Pharaoh's favor toward Sarah
had made Abraham a very wealthy man. They returned to Bethel
("the house of the Lord"), where Abraham called on the name of
the Lord with a sacrifice. Henceforth, the Lord himself would be
their dwelling place.

Note that Sarah's devotion to Abraham—a significant act of
faith under the circumstances—became the means of blessing
for both of them, in spite of her husband's cowardly scheming.
Clearly the Lord blessed Sarah's faithfulness, not Abraham's
failure. Therefore, the faith of one mitigated the foolishness of
the other.

The lesson: Do your part to be a faithful partner and trust
God to bless you both.

PHILIPPIANS 1:6

[I am] confident of this very thing, that He who has begun a good work in you will complete it until the day of Jesus Christ.

A braham was the human channel through which the world would see the outpouring of God's redemptive plan. He understood that. Sarah understood and embraced it (Hebrews 11:11). But despite her faith, she knew from a human perspective that her long years of childlessness already loomed large as a threat to the fulfillment of God's pledge. Sarah must have constantly pondered these things, and as time went by, the weight of her burden only increased.

The plan for the believer is clear. God is conforming us to the image of Christ (Romans 8:37–39; Philippians 1:6; 1 John 3:2). His power is what will accomplish this; not works or ceremonies that we carry out in our own energy. However, from a human perspective, the power of sin looms large and threatens to undermine God's plan. Avoid sin, and remain steadfastly confident in the greater power of God.

MATTHEW 19:4–6

[Jesus] answered and said to them, "Have you not read that He who made them at the beginning 'made them male and female,' and said, 'For this reason a man shall leave his father and mother and be joined to his wife, and the two shall become one flesh'? So then, they are no longer two but one flesh."

Sarah's scheme and Abraham's spineless consent became the first recorded case of polygamy in Scripture involving a righteous man. Abraham took a concubine, at his wife's urging, and this became a sorry precedent for the patriarch of the nation to set. In generations to come, Jacob would be duped by his uncle into marrying both Leah and Rachel; David would take many concubines; and Solomon would carry polygamy to an almost unbelievable extreme, maintaining a harem of more than a thousand women.

But God's design for marriage was monogamy from the beginning, and disobedience to that standard has always resulted in evil consequences. No good has ever come from any violation of the "one-flesh" principle of monogamy. Furthermore, if you are married, how you regard your union—in public and even in private—will become your children's legacy. They learn by what they experience.

*So he went in to Hagar, and she conceived. And when she saw that she had
conceived, her mistress became despised in her eyes. Then Sarai said to
Abram, "My wrong be upon you! I gave my maid into your embrace; and
when she saw that she had conceived, I became despised in her eyes. The
LORD judge between you and me."*

As soon as Sarah's handmaid conceived, Sarah knew her plan
had been a grave mistake. Here, then, is the first outburst of
temper we see from Sarah. She blamed Abraham for her misery,
which was of course unreasonable. This whole sordid plan was,
after all, her bad idea. Yes, as the spiritual head of the household,
Abraham should have rejected Sarah's plan out of hand—but it's
still not quite fair to pin all the guilt on him.

Blame shifting, especially in marriage, is as old as humanity. In
the Garden of Eden, Adam pointed to Eve, who in turn charged
the serpent. And guilt has been a hot potato ever since. When
something goes terribly wrong, be bold, own your part. Take the
lead by accepting responsibility for whatever you might have
done wrong—however small your contribution—so that relationships can mend and healing can begin.

ROMANS 5:3 – 5

We also glory in tribulations, knowing that tribulation produces
perseverance; and perseverance, character; and character, hope. Now hope
does not disappoint, because the love of God has been poured out in our
hearts by the Holy Spirit who was given to us.

Sarah's frustration was only magnified when Hagar was promised a multitude of descendants. Sarah had never received such a promise from God. Sarah's faith resided in promises God had made to Abraham. Up to this point, Sarah had never explicitly been named as the matriarch in the covenant God made with Abraham. That was her hope and expectation. But the episode with Hagar shows that Sarah's hope was beginning to wane. She was slowly losing heart.

God's timing can be difficult to accept; nevertheless, it is perfect. Aside from the fact that He wanted Sarah's pregnancy to be a miracle, He wanted to work on Sarah's heart. Unfortunately, pain is usually an indispensible part of the healing. Before her heart would be ready to receive the immense blessing He had in store, it had to be softened to the point of surrender. But because God was doing the work, her pain brought her to submission, and her submission yielded mature faith.

HEBREWS 11:11

By faith Sarah herself also received strength to conceive seed, and she bore
a child when she was past the age, because she judged Him faithful who
had promised.

Thirteen more frustrating years passed for Sarah after the birth of Hagar's son, and she remained barren. Year after year had come and gone. She was now an old woman, and no matter how often she and Abraham tried to conceive, the promise was *still* unfulfilled. Here's where the greatness of Sarah's faith shines through. Most women would have given up hope long before this. A lesser woman might have despaired of ever seeing YHWH's promise fulfilled—and perhaps even turned to paganism instead. But we are reminded again that Sarah "judged Him faithful who had promised."

Systematically through the years, everything that sustained Sarah's hope was removed—her youth, her fertility, her daydreams, her schemes—until nothing held her hope in place except her trust in the goodness and power of God. The crisis of faith for her was the same as it is for most people: Would she trust in the truth of God's Word? For her, the answer was yes.

GENESIS 17:15–16

Then God said to Abraham, "As for Sarai your wife, you shall not call her name Sarai, but Sarah shall be her name. And I will bless her and also give you a son by her; then I will bless her, and she shall be a mother of nations; kings of peoples shall be from her."

When the time finally came to fulfill His promise of a son to Abraham, the Lord then turned the subject to Sarah. For the first time on record, He specifically brought Sarah by name into the covenant promises and commanded that her name be changed from Sarai, my princess," to Sarah, "princess." By removing the possessive pronoun (*my*), the Lord was taking away the limiting aspect of her name, since she was to be ancestor to many nations.

Experience has taught me that when God allows pain to do its transforming work on a heart, the sum total of sorrow cannot compare to the immense joy He brings. The pain is never more than is absolutely necessary to prepare His beloved for the blessing He wants us to enjoy.

If you are currently struggling under a load of sorrow, endure with patience. The joy that awaits you—if not in this life, then unquestionably in the next—will be immeasurably greater than the pain you suffer now.

GENESIS 18:10, 12

And [the angel] said, "I will certainly return to you according to the time of life, and behold, Sarah your wife shall have a son." (Sarah was listening in the tent door which was behind him.) . . . Therefore Sarah laughed within herself, saying, "After I have grown old, shall I have pleasure, my lord being old also?"

The next time the Lord appeared to Abraham, one of His express purposes was to renew the promise for Sarah's sake so that she could hear it with her own ears. Sarah's laughter (just like Abraham's in 17:17) seems to have been an exclamation of joy and amazement rather than doubt. Yet when the Lord asked, "Why did Sarah laugh?" she denied it. She was afraid because she had not laughed out loud, but "within herself." The fact that the stranger knew her inner thoughts proved to her that it was the Lord.

Sarah had released her white-knuckle grip on what she felt was her right as a woman. Sarah surrendered any sense of entitlement. Sarah submitted *her* life plan to the sovereign will of God. Then— and only then—she was prepared to bear her first child, at the tender age of ninety! And she could barely contain her joy.

GENESIS 21:1-2

The LORD visited Sarah as He had said, and the LORD did for Sarah as He had spoken. For Sarah conceived and bore Abraham a son in his old age, at the set time of which God had spoken to him.

The repeated Hebrew phrase "as He had said" is no accident. The point is that God was true to His word despite Sarah's advanced, postmenopausal condition. He always fulfills His promises, which is always a source of joy. Sarah named her boy Isaac, meaning "laughter." And she said, "God has made me laugh, and all who hear will laugh with me" (21:6).

God's long-awaited promise had finally come to fruition. She endured the long trial with her faith intact, and her frustration instantly gave way to delight, pure joy, and even laughter.

That same kind of spiritual euphoria awaits every true believer at the end of life's trials. The joy of heaven must be indescribably sweet, because it never ends. "All who hear"—those who share the same faith as Sarah—will indeed laugh with her throughout eternity.

GENESIS 21:6–7

*Sarah said, "God has made me laugh, and all who hear will laugh with me."
She also said, "Who would have said to Abraham that Sarah would nurse
children? For I have borne him a son in his old age."*

We're given a fascinating insight into Sarah's real character by the fact that she saw genuine humor in the way God had dealt with her. After those long years of bitter frustration, she could still appreciate the irony and relish the comedy of becoming a mother at such an old age. Her life's ambition was now realized, and the memory of years of bitter disappointment quickly disappeared from view. God had indeed been faithful.

Scripture gives us enough insight into Sarah's character to make it clear that she was not necessarily blessed with a naturally sunny disposition or a keen sense of humor. The joy she manifested on this occasion was pure spiritual delight—a true foretaste of the happiness of heaven. This became a turning point in her life too. After a miraculous answer to prayer of this magnitude, she would never again find it easy to succumb to feelings of despair.

There's an important lesson here for all of us: when we bear in mind that God is sovereign and keep our hearts focused on His goodness, it is much easier to see beyond the trials and setbacks providence often deals us. Knowing that God's plan is always for our good (Romans 8:28) will help us maintain our joy, even in the midst of this life's difficulties.

MATTHEW 6:24

"No one can serve two masters; for either he will hate the one and love the other, or else he will be loyal to the one and despise the other. You cannot serve God and mammon."

In Scripture, the relative silence about James, the brother of John, is ironic because from a human perspective, he might have seemed the logical one to dominate the group. James was most likely older than John. And between the two sets of brothers, the family of James and John seems to have been much more prominent than the family of Peter and Andrew. James and his brother were among the few disciples to have a surname. They were known as "the sons of Zebedee."

Wealth, rank, and privilege are neither good nor evil. Like anything, such as Peter's natural bent toward leadership, they can become an asset or a liability, depending upon how the person is shaped by a skillful teacher. And in this case, James had the best.

You undoubtedly have certain tangible assets that can become either helpful or hurtful. Take some time to list them. Consider their potential impact. Then present them in prayer as a sacrifice to God.

1 PETER 3:13

Who is he who will harm you if you become followers of what is good?

If there's a key word that applies to the life of the apostle James, that word is *passion*. From the little we know about him, it is obvious that he was a man of intense fervor and intensity. In fact, Jesus gave James and his brother the nickname *Boanerges*—"Sons of Thunder." He was zealous, thunderous, passionate, and fervent.

Passion and zeal, like tangible assets, can be great assets if put to the right use. Passion is infectious and zeal spurs others into action.

What stokes the fire within you? What excites you? What positive change would you like to accomplish in your community or in the world? Very likely, that passion has been discouraged, perhaps by you more than others. Let me encourage you to give that passion an outlet. Start channeling that zeal into prayer. Direct those passionate desires heavenward. Then watch for opportunities to open up. You just wait and see!

PHILIPPIANS 3:8

Indeed I also count all things loss for the excellence of the knowledge of Christ Jesus my Lord, for whom I have suffered the loss of all things, and count them as rubbish, that I may gain Christ.

James reminds me of Jehu in the Old Testament, who was known for driving his chariot at breakneck speed and who said, "Come with me, and see my zeal for the Lord." But Jehu's passion was passion out of control, and his "zeal for the Lord" was tainted with selfish, worldly ambition and the most bloodthirsty kinds of cruelty.

James's zeal was mixed with similar ambitions and bloodthirsty tendencies (although in milder doses), and he may have been headed down a similar road to ruin when Jesus met him. By God's grace, he was transformed into a man of God and became one of the leading apostles.

As you look back over your shoulder, can you predict what you might have become were it not for Jesus? You may not have thought about the past this way before, but it's worth doing. Imagine where you might have ended up and let that fuel your praise for God's grace.

PHILIPPIANS 4:8—9

Finally, brethren, whatever things are true, whatever things are noble,
whatever things are just, whatever things are pure, whatever things are
lovely, whatever things are of good report, if there is any virtue and if there
is anything praiseworthy—meditate on these things. The things which you
learned and received and heard and saw in me, these do, and the God of
peace will be with you.

The very few specific mentions of James in Scripture underscore that he had a fiery, vehement disposition. While Andrew
was quietly bringing individuals to Jesus, James was wishing he
could call fire down from heaven to destroy whole villages of
people! James was not a passive or subtle man, but rather he had
a style that stirred things up, so that he made deadly enemies
very rapidly.

Passion can be either inspiring or inflammatory. It can breed
excitement or stir anger. Moreover, passion can multiply friends
or enemies, all depending upon what fuels that fervor. Before
Christ encountered and redirected James, his passion was fueled
by self-righteousness, not love.

As you consider what stirs your zeal and motivates you to
action, be certain it is something pleasing to God. Check to see
that your passion is true, noble, just, pure, lovely.

MATTHEW 5:14–15

"You are the light of the world. A city set on a hill cannot be hidden; nor does anyone light a lamp and put it under a basket, but on the lampstand, and it gives light to all who are in the house."

There is a legitimate place in spiritual leadership for people who have thunderous personalities. Elijah was that kind of man. Indeed, James looked to Elijah as a role model. Nehemiah was similarly passionate (cf. Nehemiah 13:25). John the Baptist had a fiery temperament too. And James was apparently cut from similar fabric. He was outspoken, intense, and impatient with evildoers.

Thank God for bold, forthright people who do not abide evil without confronting it. Their fiery response reflects the righteous wrath of God against sin and rouses us from our slumbering, complacent toleration of wrongdoing. When the passion *begins* with a hatred for sin in the thundering prophet's own heart—and as long as the prophet hates hypocrisy as much as he hates other sins—such zeal can be a powerful force for good. We could use a few prophets like that today.

Do not let your heart envy sinners,
But be zealous for the fear of the LORD all the day.

There's nothing wrong with zeal per se, but sometimes zeal is less than righteous. Zeal apart from knowledge can be damning. Zeal without wisdom is dangerous. Zeal mixed with insensitivity is often cruel. Whenever zeal disintegrates into uncontrolled passion, it can be deadly. And James sometimes had a tendency to let such misguided zeal get the better of him.

We must never forget that the Old Testament prophets received supernatural revelation from God telling them what to say and what to do. John the Baptist was set aside by God from birth to be the forerunner of the Christ. And Jesus, being God, spoke and acted unerringly. We, on the other hand, must be careful not to allow the flesh to fuel our zeal. Instead, look to Scripture for clear, unambiguous instruction. Be sure you have no boards in your own eye before you try to remove that speck from a neighbor's. Make certain your zeal is tempered and regulated by the fruit of the Spirit.

When all those things are in order, it is a *good* thing to cultivate zeal.

LUKE 9:51–53

When the days were approaching for [Jesus'] ascension, He was determined to go to Jerusalem; and He sent messengers on ahead of Him, and they went and entered a village of the Samaritans to make arrangements for Him. But they did not receive Him, because He was traveling toward Jerusalem.

The Samaritans were the mixed-race offspring of Israelites from the Northern Kingdom and transplanted pagans conquered by the Assyrians. A Hebrew priest who had been taken captive was returned to Samaria to teach people how to fear the Lord (2 Kings 17:28). The result was a religion that claimed to worship Yahweh (and ostensibly accepted the Pentateuch as Scripture), but they founded their own priesthood, built their own temple, and devised a sacrificial system of their own making. The Samaritans' religion is a classic example of what happens when the authority of Scripture is subjected to human tradition.

Religion in the West is not much different. Many supposedly Christian churches have selected from a smorgasbord of mystical beliefs and incorporated them into orthodox theology, and the result is anything but Christian.

Take a close look at the beliefs you received through tradition. Are they biblical?

JOHN 4:20–22

[The Samaritan woman said,] "Our fathers worshiped in this mountain, and you people say that in Jerusalem is the place where men ought to worship." Jesus said to her, "Woman, believe Me, an hour is coming when neither in this mountain nor in Jerusalem will you worship the Father. You worship what you do not know; we worship what we know, for salvation is from the Jews."

The original site of the Samaritans' temple on Mount Gerizim, in Samaria, was still deemed holy by the people of that region, and they were convinced the mountain was the only place where God could be worshiped properly. Obviously, this was one of the chief points under dispute between the Jews and the Samaritans. Of course, the Jews regarded the people of Samaria a mongrel race and their religion a mongrel religion. Therefore, the entire region was deemed unclean by most Jews, who preferred to add two extra days to their journey in order to go around, rather than through, Samaria.

Jesus didn't care much for nonbiblical traditions. Nor did he feel the need to avoid people the religious elite in Jerusalem detested. In fact, He made it a point to interact with the Samaritans as much as possible. He never compromised truth; He always taught it boldly. Nevertheless, He proclaimed the truth in love.

MATTHEW 5:38–39

"You have heard that it was said, 'An eye for an eye, and a tooth for a tooth.'
But I say to you, do not resist an evil person; but whoever slaps you on your
right cheek, turn the other to him also."

Along the road to Jerusalem, through Samaria, Jesus and His followers would need places to eat and spend the night. Since the party traveling with Jesus was fairly large, He sent messengers ahead to arrange accommodations. Because the Jewish group was headed to Jerusalem to celebrate the Passover, and the Samaritans were of the opinion that all feasts and ceremonies ought to be observed on Mount Gerizim, the messengers were refused all accommodations.

Hospitality to travelers remains to this day a sacred obligation in the Middle East, regardless of religion. Refusing to accommodate a traveler was considered an outrageous insult.

All of us, at one time or another, will become objects of derision, ill treatment, injustice, or even abuse. How we choose to respond will make us either more like Jesus Christ or more like our antagonist. And if we return evil for evil and sin for sin, how can we call ourselves disciples of Jesus Christ? Sometimes our best response is no response.

MATTHEW 5:44–45

"I say to you, love your enemies and pray for those who persecute you, so that you may be sons of your Father who is in heaven; for He causes His sun to rise on the evil and the good, and sends rain on the righteous and the unrighteous."

Jesus had never shown anything but goodwill toward the Samaritans, but now they were treating Him with contempt. James and his brother, the Sons of Thunder, were instantly filled with passionate outrage. They already had in mind a remedy for the situation. They recalled Elijah's experience in this very region, which was even then a hotbed of idol worship.

An idolatrous king had sent a contingent of soldiers to apprehend the prophet and bring him in for execution. When the commander addressed the prophet as "Man of God," Elijah replied, "If I am a man of God, then let fire come down from heaven and consume you and your fifty men" (2 Kings 1:10). And that's exactly what happened.

When James and John suggested fire from heaven as a fitting response to the Samaritans' inhospitality, they probably thought they were standing on solid precedent. But they were completely out of step with their Master's plan.

JOHN 3:17

"For God did not send the Son into the world to judge the world, but that the world might be saved through Him."

The time and circumstances for Elijah were unlike any other. Moreover, he acted on the explicit instructions of God, not of his own initiative. Calling down fiery destruction on the Samaritan village was not the right response for James and his brother. They were in effect asking Jesus to empower them to do their own will rather than His. And as soon as we wish for the power to carry out our will with no regard for the plans of God, we might as well establish a temple of our own making and worship how we please.

Jesus' mission was very different from Elijah's. Christ came to save, not to destroy.

When your enemies and their attacks come to mind, what is your response? In the privacy of your mind, do you call down fire from heaven? Is your plan for those difficult people the same as the Lord's? If you are to be an authentic disciple, His mission must become your mission. And that begins with a mind transformed to think like He does.

LUKE 9:55–56

But [Jesus] turned and rebuked them, and said, "You do not know what kind of spirit you are of; for the Son of Man did not come to destroy men's lives, but to save them." And they went on to another village.

Jesus severely rebuked James and his brother for their selfish, self-righteous outburst of hatred. After all this time with Jesus, how could they have missed the spirit of so much He had taught? He was on a mission of rescue, not judgment. Of course, a time is coming when Christ will judge the world. Those who do not know God "shall be punished with everlasting destruction from the presence of the Lord and from the glory of His power" (2 Thessalonians 1:7–9). But this was not the time or the place for that.

God cares very much about justice, even when it seems that He is allowing so much evil to go unanswered. The time will come when all sin will be brought to account. But not now. For now, Christ has called us to be part of His redemptive plan. That means when we are slighted or offended, we must choose to "go on to another village."

MATTHEW 18:7

"Woe to the world because of its stumbling blocks! For it is inevitable that stumbling blocks come; but woe to that man through whom the stumbling block comes!"

While James momentarily forgot that "now is the day of salvation" (2 Corinthians 6:2), there is perhaps a touch of nobility in James and John's indignation against the Samaritans. Their zeal to defend Christ's honor is surely a great virtue. It is far better to get fired up with righteous wrath than to sit passively and endure insults against Christ. So their resentment over seeing Jesus deliberately slighted is admirable in some measure, even though their reaction was tainted with arrogance and their proposed remedy was completely out of line.

You may have noticed that it has become fashionable in our culture to make fun of Jesus. He is sold in gag gift shops, lampooned in popular movies, and even featured as a cartoon sitcom character. And it's only going to get worse. Our response will be increasingly important because the world is watching. Will we try to call down fire from heaven? Or will we continue to proclaim the gospel with a dignity that honors our Lord?

ACTS 8:5−6, 8

Philip went down to the city of Samaria and began proclaiming Christ to them. The crowds with one accord were giving attention to what was said by Philip, as they heard and saw the signs which he was performing. . . . So there was much rejoicing in that city.

Instant destruction would be fitting every time anyone sinned, if that were how God chose to deal with us. But thankfully, it ordinarily is not. "His tender mercies are over all His works" (Psalm 145:9). Jesus' example taught James that loving-kindness and mercy are virtues to be cultivated as much as (and sometimes more than) righteous indignation and fiery zeal.

A few years later, Phillip the deacon "went down to the city of Samaria and preached Christ to them" (Acts 8:5). Multitudes responded positively and heeded his invitation to accept Christ. And we can be certain that even James himself rejoiced greatly in the salvation of so many who once had dishonored Christ so flagrantly.

People frequently regret saying or doing something in the heat of fiery zeal; they rarely regret exercising restraint.

MATTHEW 20:20–21

Then the mother of the sons of Zebedee came to Jesus with her sons, bowing down and making a request of Him. And He said to her, "What do you wish?" She said to Him, "Command that in Your kingdom these two sons of mine may sit one on Your right and one on Your left."

J ames was not only fervent, passionate, zealous, and insensitive; he was also ambitious and overconfident. And in this case, he and his brother John engaged in a furtive attempt to gain status over the other apostles. They colluded with their mother, Salome (Matthew 27:56, Mark 16:1), to make the most of Jesus' earlier promise: "When the Son of Man sits on the throne of His glory, you who have followed Me will also sit on twelve thrones, judging the twelve tribes of Israel" (Matthew 19:28). They probably put forward their mother to speak on their behalf because of the family's affluence and social standing.

Unfortunately, even churches are sometimes characterized by that kind of maneuvering for clout and political advantage. Some churches choose their leaders by singling out whoever has achieved the most material prosperity in secular business. As a result, their leaders may or may not be spiritual men who maintain a close walk with the Lord. But the Lord isn't impressed by worldly clout; He wants servants—humble, unassuming, authentic slaves.

MARK 10:38–39

But Jesus said to them, "You do not know what you are asking. Are you able to drink the cup that I drink, or to be baptized with the baptism with which I am baptized?" They said to Him, "We are able." And Jesus said to them, "The cup that I drink you shall drink; and you shall be baptized with the baptism with which I am baptized."

James and John were already in the intimate circle of three. They had been disciples as long as anyone. They probably thought of numerous reasons why they deserved this honor, so why not simply ask for it? Obviously Salome had encouraged her sons' ambition. Jesus' reply subtly reminded them that suffering is the prelude to glory, but they had no real concept of what was stirring in the cup He was asking them to drink. So, of course, in their foolish, ambitious self-confidence, they assured Him, "We are able."

How often we ask for what we think we want but have no concept of what we're asking. In fact, there have been times I was thankful the Lord denied my request, after seeing things in 20/20 hindsight! Fortunately, God knows all. He is never surprised by our requests, and He knows what's best for us better than we do. He ultimately granted the request of James and John; their suffering did indeed reap great glory.

MARK 10:43-44

"Whoever wishes to become great among you shall be your servant; and whoever wishes to be first among you shall be slave of all."

James wanted a crown of glory; Jesus gave him a cup of suffering. He wanted power; Jesus gave him servanthood. He wanted a place of prominence; Jesus gave him a martyr's grave. He wanted to rule; Jesus gave him a sword—not to wield, but to be the instrument of his own execution.

James received virtually everything he asked for and more. For in the new kingdom, suffering *is* the way to glory, the most powerful place goes to the lowest slave, and there is no greater prominence than a martyr's epitaph. James drank of Christ's cup when he stood alone before Herod Agrippa I and became the first of the Twelve to be killed for his faith. Now, the glory, power, and distinction he enjoys exceed the capacity of words to describe.

So may it be for you and me. But first, we must drink of His cup.

LUKE 6:22–23

"Blessed are you when men hate you, and ostracize you, and insult you, and scorn your name as evil, for the sake of the Son of Man. Be glad in that day and leap for joy, for behold, your reward is great in heaven. For in the same way their fathers used to treat the prophets."

It is significant that James was the first of the apostles to be killed. Clearly, he was still a man of passion. His passion, now under the Holy Spirit's control, had been so instrumental in the spread of the truth that it had aroused the wrath of Herod. Obviously, James was right where he had always hoped to be and where Christ had trained him to be—on the front line as the gospel advanced and the church grew.

I am amazed by the Lord's ability to completely transform a person, transform our nature without destroying our identity. James completely changed, but he remained the same passionate, zealous disciple.

Don't fear submitting yourself to God's metamorphosis. Don't fear losing your edge or sacrificing your happiness. What you gain in the end is a greater, more complete conformity to the likeness of Christ and more joy than you can contain.

ACTS 12:1-2

Now about that time Herod the king laid hands on some who belonged to the church in order to mistreat them. And he had James the brother of John put to death with a sword.

James the Son of Thunder had been mentored by Christ, empowered by the Holy Spirit, and shaped by those means into a man whose zeal and ambition were useful instruments in the hands of God for the spreading of the kingdom. Still courageous, zealous, and committed to the truth, he had apparently learned to use those qualities for the Lord's service, rather than for his own aggrandizement. And now his strength was so great that when Herod decided it was time to stop the church, James was the first man he thought to kill.

James is the prototype of the passionate, zealous front-runner who is dynamic, strong, and ambitious. Ultimately, his passions were tempered by sensitivity and grace. And the Lord used him to do a wonderful work in the early church. His life was relatively short, but his influence continues to this day.

COLOSSIANS 4:5–6

Conduct yourselves with wisdom toward outsiders, making the most of the opportunity. Let your speech always be with grace, as though seasoned with salt, so that you will know how you should respond to each person.

If I have to choose between a man of burning, flaming, passionate enthusiasm with a potential for failure on the one hand, and a cold compromiser on the other hand, I'll take the man with passion every time. Such zeal must always be harnessed and tempered with love. But if it is surrendered to the control of the Holy Spirit and blended with patience and long-suffering, such zeal is a marvelous instrument in the hands of God. The life of James offers clear proof of that.

If you are a person of passion and zeal, your potential for the kingdom is immense. The danger is that you will pursue the wrong object with good motives or, just as tragic, pursue the right object with poor motives. So let me encourage you to submit yourself to the mentoring of an Andrew-like disciple. Commit to remaining accountable and to trusting his or her discernment. That will be difficult, but you will undoubtedly be grateful in the long run.

By faith the harlot Rahab did not perish with those who did not believe,
when she had received the spies with peace.

The Lord had ordered the destruction of many Canaanite cities for the same reason He personally destroyed Sodom and Gomorrah: the inhabitants were so incorrigibly dedicated to their sin that no hope of their repentance existed (Genesis 18:23–33). Because God knows the heart of each person intimately and knows the future of every potential decision, He could make that determination.

As far as we know, Rahab had always been a willing participant in her civilization's trademark debauchery. She had personally profited from the evil that permeated that whole society. Now that God had called for the complete destruction of the entire culture, why shouldn't Rahab also receive just punishment for her own deliberate sin? No one knows for certain. All we know for sure is that while Rachel's sin was no less despicable, the Lord nevertheless arranged for her preservation during the coming siege and then her salvation from sin. We also know it was not due to any merit of her own.

JOSHUA 2:1

Now Joshua the son of Nun sent out two men from Acacia Grove to spy secretly, saying, "Go, view the land, especially Jericho." So they went, and came to the house of a harlot named Rahab, and lodged there.

Rahab lived in Jericho, which was part of the Amorite kingdom, a grotesquely violent, totally depraved, thoroughly pagan culture so hell-bent on the pursuit of everything evil that God had condemned them and ordered the Israelites to wipe them from the face of the earth (Deuteronomy 20:17). As a prostitute, Rahab epitomized the vileness of the Amorite culture at a point when they had collectively filled the measure of human wickedness to its very brim. Yet God meticulously orchestrated her salvation through circumstances that many would think coincidental. But it isn't the Lord's way to leave any soul subject to the whims of coincidence.

If you have trusted in Jesus Christ and received His free gift of eternal life, your salvation was no accident. While living in a world that is under God's sentence of condemnation—indeed, marked out for *eternal* destruction—the Lord sought you out. He orchestrated events to redeem you and to liberate you.

"Ah, Lord GOD! Behold, You have made the heavens and the earth by Your great power and outstretched arm. There is nothing too hard for You. You show lovingkindness to thousands, and repay the iniquity of the fathers into the bosom of their children after them—the Great, the Mighty God, whose name is the LORD of hosts.'"

Rahab is the very first person Scripture introduces us to in the Promised Land. By God's gracious providence, her whole life, her career, and her future would be changed by her surprise encounter with two Hebrew spies. Their collaboration with Rahab was the beginning of the downfall of Jericho, the first dramatic conquest in one of history's greatest military campaigns ever.

This encounter with Rahab reveals several truths concerning the character of God and how He chose to give the Promised Land to Israel. First, she illustrates the fact that anyone willing to receive the Hebrews would be spared and then received into the family of God. Second, God was willing to forgive the sin of any who repented. Third, the Canaanites condemned themselves by refusing to repent. And, finally, *nothing* was going to prevent God from accomplishing His will.

Clearly, some things never change.

1 PETER 3:15

Sanctify the Lord God in your hearts, and always be ready to give a defense to everyone who asks you a reason for the hope that is in you, with meekness and fear.

The Israelite spies did not seek out Rahab to take advantage of her for immoral purposes, of course. Perhaps that very thing is what first won them her trust. They were obviously not there to use or abuse her, unlike virtually all the other men she ever saw. They were serious and sober, but that did not seem to frighten her in any way. Presumably, they treated her with patient dignity and respect while they made their careful reconnaissance. No doubt they explained who they were and something about YHWH as well.

Interestingly, the spies were not in Jericho to evangelize the city. However, in the course of doing as God had instructed them, the men behaved as godly men should and made the Lord a routine topic of conversation. Consequently, a ready heart responded. Come to think of it, that's a model of evangelism that might work well wherever you happen to live or work.

JOSHUA 2:5–6

[Rahab told the king of Jericho], "It happened as the gate was being shut, when it was dark, that the men went out. Where the men went I do not know; pursue them quickly, for you may overtake them." (But she had brought them up to the roof and hidden them with the stalks of flax, which she had laid in order on the roof.)

Rahab's response to the spies is surprising. There was probably a handsome reward in it for her if she turned in the spies. But she didn't. She hid them. She misdirected the officials and saved the lives of the men, even though this put her at considerable risk. Her sudden decision to help the spies, therefore, is not only unexpected; it seems to run counter to every instinct that normally would motivate a woman like Rahab. Obviously, something important had occurred within her—something supernatural in origin. Her heart had become fertile ground for the seed of God's grace, and she responded in faith.

Essentially, that's how evangelism works. God prepares the heart, we faithfully share the good news, and a soul is reborn. It isn't the clever logic of the presentation or the artful tugging of heartstrings that brings someone to faith. It's the supernatural work of God. But He graciously uses our faithfulness and our testimony to accomplish His purpose.

HEBREWS 11:31

By faith the harlot Rahab did not perish with those who did not believe,
when she had received the spies with peace.

Rahab's actions in protecting the spies involved the telling of a lie. Was that justified? By commending her for her faith, is Scripture also condoning her methods? There's no need for clever rationalization to try to justify her lie. Scripture never commends *the lie*. Rahab isn't applauded for her *ethics*. Rahab is a positive example of *faith*. Her faith was, at the time, newborn, weak, in need of nurture and growth. She knew enough about YHWH to trust Him, but that trust was still far from perfect.

All believers grow and progress in sanctification. People don't spring full grown into spiritual maturity. God is patient with us, strengthening our faith and conforming us to the likeness of His Son despite our weaknesses. Sometimes He even uses our failures to accomplish His will. That doesn't justify our sin, of course, but it demonstrates one important way in which His strength is made perfect in weakness, and it reminds us of the sufficiency and necessity of His grace (cf. 2 Corinthians 12:9).

We must acknowledge our failures and repent of them—but then we press toward the goal of perfection (Philippians 3:14), "forgetting those things which are behind and reaching forward to those things which are ahead" (v. 13).

JAMES 2:25–26

Was not Rahab the harlot also justified by works when she received the messengers and sent them out another way? For as the body without the spirit is dead, so faith without works is dead also.

While Rahab's faith was undeveloped—as one would expect of a new believer—it nevertheless bore the fruit of action immediately. She "received the spies with peace" (Hebrews 11:31)—meaning that she not only hid them, but also implicitly embraced their cause. She thereby entrusted her whole future to their God. Nothing but faith could have made such a dramatic, instantaneous change in the character of such a woman.

Genuine faith—even the immature faith of a new believer—will immediately manifest itself in changed behavior. The transformation in one's conduct may be slow-moving, gradual, and unsteady, but the behavior of a genuine believer nonetheless testifies that a change has occurred within. If your conduct is not becoming more godly over time, something is terribly wrong in your spiritual walk. Your relationship with the Lord is not as it should be.

"As soon as we heard [about the Exodus], our hearts melted; neither did there remain any more courage in anyone because of you, for the LORD your God, He is God in heaven above and on earth beneath. Now therefore, I beg you, swear to me by the Lord, since I have shown you kindness, that you also will show kindness to my father's house, and give me a true token."

Notice that Rahab's faith was accompanied by *fear*. There is nothing wrong with that. She had heard powerful evidence of the Lord's supremacy over Egypt and two fearsome Amorite kings. She probably understood something of YHWH's sovereign authority over Israel from the tales of their forty years in the wilderness. Hers was a healthy kind of fear. It led her to ask for amnesty, whereas the fear of her countrymen led them to take up arms against His people.

Everyone is right to fear God. (They should if they don't!) Scripture says "The fear of the LORD is the beginning of wisdom" (Proverbs 9:10). On the other hand, "perfect love casts out fear" (1 John 4:18). From the time when we first lay down our weapons of rebellion and take refuge in Him, we begin to discover that all the reasons we ever had for fearing God are the very reasons we can rest confident in His loving care. As we grow in the realization that nothing can separate us from His love (Romans 8:8–39), that sense of fear, now tempered by love, matures into the profoundest kind of reverence.

JOSHUA 6:20

So the people shouted when the priests blew the trumpets. And it happened when the people heard the sound of the trumpet, and the people shouted with a great shout, that the wall fell down flat. Then the people went up into the city, every man straight before him, and they took the city.

Israel's miraculous victory over Jericho is a familiar account to most people. God demolished the massive walls of Jericho without any military means whatsoever. Only one part of the wall was spared. The section that housed Rahab had been marked by a scarlet cord, and when the dust settled, Joshua ordered the two spies to "go into the harlot's house, and from there bring out the woman and all that she has, as you swore to her." Rahab is a marvelous illustration of how the Lord can simultaneously wipe out evil and spare the few who seek refuge in Him.

Someday future, Christ will return to the earth. The forces of evil will vainly arm themselves for conflict, but the power they face cannot be stopped with guns or missiles. When the dust settles, nothing will remain intact except those who have taken refuge in Christ by faith. If He were to return today, how would *your* house fare?

Joshua spared Rahab the harlot, her father's household, and all that she had.
So she dwells in Israel to this day, because she hid the messengers whom
Joshua sent to spy out Jericho.

Rahab is a beautiful example of the transforming power of faith. Although she had few spiritual advantages and little knowledge of the truth, her heart was drawn to YHWH. She risked her life, turned her back on a way of life that did not honor God, and from that day on lived a completely different kind of life, as a true hero of faith.

Perhaps you can identify with Rahab. Perhaps you were redeemed out of difficult or even shameful circumstances, against all odds. If so, you are in good company. From a human perspective, the genealogy of Christ is checkered with foreigners, outcasts, examples of failure, and pariahs for various reasons, all of whom underscore how scandal colored so much of the messianic line. Still, they all found a place in the plan of God to bring His Son into the world. Their place in salvation history is no accident. Christ became an outcast to redeem the outcast.

2 CORINTHIANS 5:17

If anyone is in Christ, he is a new creation; old things have passed away;
behold, all things have become new.

After the account of Jericho's destruction in Joshua 6, Rahab is never again mentioned in the Old Testament. Joshua's postscript tells us she lived out her life in quiet dignity and grace among the people of God. She was wholly changed from the kind of woman she once had been. She was, and is still, a living symbol of the transforming effect of saving faith. In fact, when we do meet Rahab again in the pages of Scripture, it is in the New Testament. Her name is mentioned three times. Two of those honor her for remarkable faith (Hebrews 11:31; James 2:25).

It's a shame that Rahab's name will always be linked with the identifier, "the harlot." That may have been what she once was, but that's not who God sees today. She is His beloved daughter, redeemed and pure—a woman of true faith. Perhaps we should call her instead Rahab the faithful.

Salmon begot Boaz by Rahab, Boaz begot Obed by Ruth, Obed begot Jesse, and Jesse begot David the king. David the king begot Solomon by her who had been the wife of Uriah.

The most amazing and delightful occurrence of Rahab's name in the New Testament is in the very first paragraph of the first gospel. Matthew began his account of Christ's life with a lengthy genealogy tracing the entire lineage of Jesus from the time of Abraham. Matthew's goal, of course, was to prove by Jesus' pedigree that He qualified to be the promised Seed of Abraham, and that he is also rightful heir to the Davidic throne.

Rahab's rags-to-righteousness story epitomizes the lavish grace of God on those who trust Him. The Lord knew her heart and knew her future. He had chosen her before creation ever began. And when the time was right, He sent two spies on an errand—yes to scout the Promised Land—but also to retrieve His beloved Rahab from the fringes of pagan society. He then gave her the great honor of being a forebear of both King David and the Messiah.

ROMANS 6:5-7

*For if we have been united together in the likeness of His death, certainly
we also shall be in the likeness of His resurrection, knowing this, that our
old man was crucified with Him, that the body of sin might be done away
with, that we should no longer be slaves of sin. For he who has died has been
freed from sin.*

Some of the scholastic rabbis just prior to Jesus' time became
embarrassed by the fact that a woman with Rahab's background was spared destruction and brought into Israel as a proselyte. They proposed a different understanding of the Hebrew
word for *harlot*, which is similar to a word meaning "to feed."
They suggested she was merely an innkeeper. Unfortunately,
the Hebrew word can mean only one thing: "harlot." In the
Septuagint, the Greek term is *porne*, from which we derive our
word *pornography*.

The biblical record doesn't need sanitizing. Remove the stigma
of sin, and you remove the need for grace. Rahab is extraordinary
precisely because she received extraordinary grace. The disturbing fact about what she once was simply magnifies the glory of
divine grace, which is what made her the extraordinary woman
she became—just like the disciples! That, after all, is the whole
lesson of her life.

JOHN 15:5

*"I am the vine, you are the branches; he who abides in Me and I in him, he
bears much fruit, for apart from Me you can do nothing."*

Almost everything we observed about the personality and
character of James is also true of John, the younger half of
the Boanerges Brothers duo. The two men had similar tempera-
ments, and they were inseparable in the gospel accounts. John was
right there with James, eager to call down fire from heaven against
the Samaritans. He was also in the thick of the debates about who
was the greatest. His zeal and ambition mirrored that of his elder
brother. Therefore, it is all the more remarkable that John has often
been nicknamed "the apostle of love."

Perhaps you have a character trait or two that have given you
more trouble than joy. If so, you will be encouraged by the life of
John. If this Son of Thunder can become the church's foremost
authority on Christian love, then there is hope for all of us!
Remain close to Christ as he did, and the Lord will do the rest.

OUR PERFECT WEAKNESS

2 CORINTHIANS 12:9

And He said to me, "My grace is sufficient for you, for My strength is made
perfect in weakness." Therefore most gladly I will rather boast in my
infirmities, that the power of Christ may rest upon me.

While John was capable of behaving in the most sectarian, narrow-minded, unbending, reckless, and impetuous fashion, he nevertheless aged well. Under the control of the Holy Spirit, all his liabilities were exchanged for assets. Compare the young disciple to the aged patriarch, and you'll see that as he matured, his areas of greatest weakness developed into his greatest strengths. He eventually became a tenderhearted elder statesman of the early church, universally loved and respected for his devotion to Christ—allowing the Lord's strength to be made perfect in his weakness.

Take a few moments now to reflect on your own character and identify what you consider to be your greatest weakness. It's usually something that has made life difficult for you for many years. Present that to the Lord in prayer as a sacrifice and ask Him to demonstrate His strength through that particular weakness. He will be faithful to hear and to answer. We have his promise.

1 JOHN 3:18

My little children, let us not love in word or in tongue, but in deed and in truth.

Love did not nullify the apostle John's passion for truth. Rather, it gave him the balance he needed. He retained to the end of his life a deep and abiding love for God's truth. In fact, this zeal for truth shaped the way he wrote. Of all the writers in the New Testament, he is the most black and white in his thinking. He thought and wrote in absolutes with very few gray areas in his teaching. He divided the world into two categories: Light and darkness, truth and lies, life and death, love and fear, children of God and children of Satan. He understood the need to present truth using clear lines of distinction.

Love need not compromise truth. We often try to "love" people by hiding or disguising difficult truths, but this isn't necessary. Love and truth are never enemies; they must always go together. Love without truth is deception; truth without love is a weapon.

EPHESIANS 4:14–15

We should no longer be children, tossed to and fro and carried about with
every wind of doctrine, by the trickery of men, in the cunning craftiness of
deceitful plotting, but, speaking the truth in love, may grow up in all things
into Him who is the head—Christ.

The way John wrote was a reflection of his personality. Truth
was his passion, and he went to great lengths to present truth
clearly. He wrote in black-and-white, absolute, certain terms, and
he wasted no ink coloring in all the gray areas. He gave rules of
thumb without listing all the exceptions. He left it to Paul to help
us deal with exceptions and help us recover from failure. John
always wrote with a warm, personal, pastoral tone—a reflection of
his transformed character—but what he wrote doesn't make for
soothing reading. How appropriate that his gentle manner of stating the truth should be so challenging without being harsh.

One can be uncompromising—even passionately so—while
retaining a gentle manner. And how much more effective the message! As you represent Jesus Christ to those who might be hostile
to spiritual truth, follow John's example. His message is clear, passionate, and uncompromising, but permeated with love.

PROVERBS 27:6

Faithful are the wounds of a friend,
But the kisses of an enemy are deceitful.

It is probably fair to say that one of the dangerous tendencies for a man with John's personality is that he would have a natural inclination to push things to the extremes. And indeed, it does seem that John in his younger years was a bit of an extremist. He seemed to lack a sense of spiritual equilibrium. His zeal, his sectarianism, his intolerance, and his selfish ambition were all sins of *imbalance.* They were all potential virtues, pushed to sinful extremes. That is why the greatest strengths of his character sometimes ironically caused his most prominent failures. His best characteristics frequently became pitfalls for him.

Perhaps the people who love you most and care most about your success have seen the same tendency in you. Let me encourage you to ask one or two of them this question: "What is my greatest strength and how do you see it causing trouble for me?" Then *listen.* Don't defend, don't rebut, don't react. *Listen.*

But as for you, speak the things which are proper for sound doctrine: that the older men be sober, reverent, temperate, sound in faith, in love, in patience.

We *all* fall prey to the effect of human depravity that turns our best characteristics into sinful behavior. It is wonderful to have a high regard for the truth, but zeal for the truth must be balanced by a love for people, or it can give way to judgmentalism, harshness, and a lack of compassion. It is fine to be hardworking and ambitious, but if ambition is not balanced with humility, it becomes sinful pride—self-promotion at the expense of others. Confidence is a wonderful virtue, too, but when confidence becomes a sinful *self*-confidence, we typically become smug and spiritually careless.

These virtues, when controlled by us, can only become troublesome over time. They must be submitted to the control of the Holy Spirit. How does that happen? Voluntarily. Begin by exercising restraint, which will feel awkward and restrictive at first. Remain in continual conversation with the Father and then act only when compelled. This isn't a perfect formula, but it's a good beginning.

MATTHEW 4:21–22

Going on from there, He saw two other brothers, James the son of Zebedee, and John his brother, in the boat with Zebedee their father, mending their nets. He called them, and immediately they left the boat and their father, and followed Him.

Three years with Jesus began to transform a self-centered fanatic into a mature man of balance. Three years with Jesus moved this Son of Thunder toward becoming an apostle of love. At the very points where he was most imbalanced, Christ gave him equilibrium, and in the process John was transformed from a bigoted hothead into a loving, godly elder statesman for the early church. It all began with a difficult, yet uncomplicated decision: follow Jesus or remain where he was.

The Savior has extended the same invitation to you: "Follow Me." Have you yielded to His call to become His disciple? Have you received His free gift of eternal life? If you haven't made that crucial first act of surrender to Him, nothing else you do will matter in eternity.

Don't delay. Receive His gift of grace and allow Him to begin the process of change within you.

JOHN 1:35-37

John [the Baptist] stood with two of his disciples. And looking at Jesus as He walked, he said, "Behold the Lamb of God!" The two disciples heard him speak, and they followed Jesus.

John appears to have been committed to the truth very early in life. From the beginning we see him as a spiritually aware man who sought to know and follow the truth. When we first encounter John, both he and Andrew are disciples of John the Baptist. This rugged prophet in the wilderness had said from the start that he was not the Messiah, but the one who had been called to point the way to God's incarnate Truth. So no one—least of all the Baptizer—was surprised when Andrew and John proceeded in the direction he pointed. Without hesitation the two began following Jesus.

What guides your selection of a church? Is it the crowd it attracts? The networking possibilities? The variety of entertaining programs and activities? The popularity of its pastor? Or do you crave the truth of Jesus Christ? Do you hunger for faithful exposition of the Scriptures?

3 JOHN 4

I have no greater joy than to hear that my children walk in truth.

John's love for truth is evident in all his writings. He uses the Greek word for truth twenty-five times in his gospel and twenty more times in his epistles. His strongest epithet for someone who claimed to be a believer while walking in darkness was to describe the person as "a liar, and the truth is not in him" (1 John 2:4). He correctly understood that truth is not an abstract concept. For him, truth *is* as truth *does*. Knowledge of the truth is nothing unless it produces behavior to match.

It is not enough for us to *want* truth or even to *know* truth. We must *live* truth. If someone were to evaluate your dedication to truth with nothing more to go on than your bank records and your calendar, what kind of person would they see? Perhaps now would be a good time for you to do that evaluation.

MARK 9:38–40

Now John answered Him, saying, "Teacher, we saw someone who does not follow us casting out demons in Your name, and we forbade him because he does not follow us." But Jesus said, "Do not forbid him, for no one who works a miracle in My name can soon afterward speak evil of Me. For he who is not against us is on our side."

Sometimes in his younger years, John's zeal for truth was lacking in love and compassion for people. He frequently displayed an appalling intolerance, elitism, and lack of genuine love. In one particular instance, he forbade a man to minister in the name of Jesus "because he does not follow us." The man was not officially a member of the group. Interestingly, this incident happened soon after John and the other disciples were powerless to cast out a demon (9:17–19).

Carrying the right membership card gives us neither exclusive access to the truth of God nor grants us the power to put truth into action. Some organizations and some groups align themselves with truth more effectively than others, but no one has a corner on it except God. He is the source of truth, not any particular human institution.

Carefully examine those who claim authority. If they claim to speak with divine authority based on any source other than Scripture, run—do not walk—to the nearest exit!

[Jesus] said to them, "Assuredly, I say to you that there are some standing here who will not taste death till they see the kingdom of God present with power."

O f course, that sounded to the disciples like a promise that the millennial kingdom would come in their lifetimes. Yet even today, we're still waiting for the establishment of the millennial kingdom on earth. So what was this promise about? Within a few days, John and two others received a taste of that coming glory as Christ took them to a mountain and pulled back the veil of His human flesh so that the radiant *shekinah* light blazed brilliantly, revealing a glimpse of His divine essence. (Any greater display would have incinerated the men.)

The disciples—James, John, and Peter in particular—were constantly arguing about who was the greatest among them and who should receive the greatest glory in the coming kingdom. Pride is a relentless disease.

We can only imagine how dwarfed they must have felt upon seeing *real* glory The men were forever changed by the experience.

MARK 9:9-10

Now as they came down from the mountain, He commanded them that they should tell no one the things they had seen, till the Son of Man had risen from the dead. So they kept this word to themselves, questioning what the rising from the dead meant.

The transfiguration of Christ was an amazing experience for John and the other two men to behold. They were given a unique privilege, unparalleled in the annals of redemptive history. But Jesus commanded them to keep the truth they had seen private for the time being. Can you imagine how difficult that would have been? They had to remain silent about the most amazing thing any person had ever seen! It was a formidable restraint put upon them, especially when you consider the ammunition it gave them in the disciples' scramble for supremacy.

The Bible likens truth to a sword; however, it is not a weapon to use against people. Evil is the foe; untruth binds people who desperately need rescuing. That's why truth and love must always go together.

The Lord entrusted John, James, and Peter with an incredibly powerful weapon against evil. How they handled it would become an opportunity for Jesus to prepare them for the immense responsibilities that lay in their future.

MARK 9:35-37

And [Jesus] sat down, called the twelve, and said to them, "If anyone desires to be first, he shall be last of all and servant of all." Then He took a little child and set him in the midst of them. And when He had taken him in His arms, He said to them, "Whoever receives one of these little children in My name receives Me; and whoever receives Me, receives not Me but Him who sent Me."

Shortly after the transfiguration experience, the disciples were again arguing over who was the greatest and would therefore occupy the most important positions in the new kingdom. Jesus then seized upon the opportunity to teach them once again.

The disciples' view of authority and greatness was upside-down. If they wanted to be first in the kingdom, they needed to be servants. If they wanted to be truly great, they needed to be more childlike. Instead of arguing and fighting with each other, instead of putting one another down, instead of rejecting each other and exalting themselves, they needed to take a role of a servant.

The world obviously doesn't work this way, which means we must choose our paths: Upward in the world, which is downward according to the kingdom, or upward in the kingdom, which will reap the derision of the world. There is no middle way.

EPHESIANS 4:14–15

We should no longer be children, tossed to and fro and carried about with every wind of doctrine, by the trickery of men, in the cunning craftiness of deceitful plotting, but, speaking the truth in love, may grow up in all things into Him who is the head—Christ.

The Gospels show John to be anything but a passive personality. He was aggressive. He was competitive. He condemned a man who was ministering in the name of Jesus, just because the man wasn't part of the group. John actually stepped in and tried to shut down this man's ministry for no other reason than this.

Soon after Jesus' lesson on greatness, John confessed his sectarian jealousy to Jesus, perhaps because his conscience was bothering him. His confession suggests that a transformation was taking place within him. He was being tenderized. He had always been zealous and passionate for the truth, but now the Lord was teaching him to love.

As we review our spiritual journey, we should be able to see a growing level of spiritual maturity. In fact, it should be noticeable to others. Try asking a trusted spiritual companion the following question: "What is the most significant area of growth you have seen in me over time?"

ROMANS 12:9

Let love be without hypocrisy. Abhor what is evil. Cling to what is good.

John was always committed to truth, and there's certainly nothing wrong with that, but it is not enough. Zeal for the truth must be balanced by love for people. Truth without love has no *decency*; it's just brutality. On the other hand, love without truth has no character; it's just *hypocrisy*.

Many people are just as imbalanced as John was, only in the other direction. They place too much emphasis on the love side of the fulcrum. Some are merely ignorant; others are deceived; still others simply don't care about what is true. When truth is missing, all they have is error, clothed in shallow, tolerant sentimentality.

Love must be based on a shared desire for truth, a shared desire for truth builds trust, and trust provides the foundation for relationship. Remove truth from the equation and a relationship is impossible.

1 JOHN 2:4−5

He who says, "I know Him," and does not keep His commandments, is a liar, and the truth is not in him. But whoever keeps His word, truly the love of God is perfected in him. By this we know that we are in Him.

While some try to love without truth, there are many who have all their theological ducks in a row and know their doctrine but are unloving and self-exalting. They are left with truth as cold facts, stifling and unattractive. Their lack of love cripples the power of the truth they profess to revere. Therefore, the truly godly person must cultivate both virtues in equal proportions, or else their wealth of knowledge will have no positive impact in the kingdom. And what a waste that would be.

If you could wish for anything in your sanctification, if you pursue anything in the spiritual realm, pursue a perfect balance of love with truth. Know the truth, and uphold it in love.

The Elder, to the elect lady and her children, whom I love in truth, and not only I, but also all those who have known the truth.

As a mature apostle, John learned the Lord's lessons well. His brief second epistle offers vivid proof of how well he balanced the twin virtues of truth and love. Throughout that epistle, John repeatedly coupled the concepts. In fact, the first half of the letter is spent urging his readers to walk in love. Then he balanced that emphasis on love in the second half of the epistle by urging them not to compromise love by receiving and blessing false teachers who undermine the truth. That because genuine love is, above all, discerning. Mature believers protect the people they love from falsehood, because lies and deception are deadly.

People need an environment that is permeated with truth; they thrive on honest interaction. So, wherever you find yourself, cultivate a spirit of openness in which truth can be candidly discussed and thoroughly examined. Allow no pretending. Address falsehood forthrightly and without delay. Only in truth can love flourish.

2 JOHN 10–11

*If anyone comes to you and does not bring [sound] doctrine, do not
receive him into your house nor greet him; for he who greets him shares
in his evil deeds.*

While John learned his lesson and was no longer calling
down fire from heaven against the enemies of truth, he did
strongly caution believers not to go to the other extreme. We are
not to open our homes or even bestow verbal blessings on people
who make a living twisting Scripture and opposing the truth. Nor
should we send them our money when they appear on television.

The apostle was not urging believers to be unkind or abusive
to anyone. We are commanded to do good to those who persecute us, be kind to those who hate us, bless those who oppose us,
and pray for those who despitefully use us (Luke 6:27–28). But
our blessing on our enemies must stop short of encouraging or
assisting a false teacher who is corrupting the gospel.

"Whoever desires to become great among you shall be your servant. And whoever of you desires to be first shall be slave of all. For even the Son of Man did not come to be served, but to serve, and to give His life a ransom for many."

In his youth, John had some ambitious plans for himself. It is not inherently wrong to aspire to have influence or desire success. But it is wrong to have selfish motives, as John apparently did. And it is especially wrong to be ambitious without also being humble. Ambition without humility becomes egotism, or even megalomania.

There was nothing intrinsically wrong with James and John's desire to sit next to Jesus in the kingdom. Who wouldn't desire that? And Jesus didn't rebuke them for their desire per se. Their error was in desiring *to obtain* the position more than they desired *to be worthy* of such a position. Their ambition was untempered by humility. Jesus had repeatedly made it clear that the highest positions in the kingdom are reserved for the humblest saints on earth.

MARK 9:36–37

Then He took a little child and set him in the midst of them. And when He
had taken him in His arms, He said to them, "Whoever receives one of
these little children in My name receives Me; and whoever receives Me,
receives not Me but Him who sent Me."

Christ Himself was the perfection of true humility. Furthermore, His kingdom is advanced by humble service, not by politics, status, power, or dominion. This was Jesus' whole point when He set the child in the midst of the disciples and talked to them about the childlikeness of the true believer.

In the ancient Near East, children were not seen as particularly valuable except for their future potential for labor or defense. Children are more helpless than helpful; until they come of age, they contribute nothing to society. Therefore, anyone who receives a child—that is, "to welcome" or "to treat hospitably"—cannot be motivated by selfish gain.

This, according to Jesus, is a good measure of humility. How often do you extend kindness to another when you have nothing to gain as compared to the times you derive some kind of benefit?

JOHN 19:26-27

When Jesus therefore saw His mother, and the disciple whom He loved standing by, He said to His mother, "Woman, behold your son!" Then He said to the disciple, "Behold your mother!" And from that hour that disciple took her to his own home.

John did eventually learn the balance between ambition and humility. In fact, humility is one of the great virtues that comes through in his writings.

Throughout John's gospel, for instance, he never once mentions his own name. The apostle refuses to speak of himself in reference to himself. Instead, he speaks of himself in reference to Jesus. He never paints himself in the foreground as a hero, but uses every reference to himself to honor Christ. Rather than write his own name, which might focus attention on him, he refers to himself as "the disciple whom Jesus loved," giving glory to Jesus for having loved such a man. In fact, he seems utterly in awe of the marvel that Christ loved him. He was gripped by this reality and utterly humbled by it.

For a good dose of humility, spend some time reflecting on the immense love Christ demonstrated for you by dying in your place and by continuing to bless you despite your failures.

REVELATION 1:9

I, John, both your brother and companion in the tribulation and kingdom and patience of Jesus Christ, was on the island that is called Patmos for the word of God and for the testimony of Jesus Christ.

John's humility comes through his writings in the gentle way he appeals to his readers in every one of his epistles. He calls them "little children," "beloved"—and he includes himself as a brother and fellow child of God. There's a tenderness and compassion in those expressions that shows his humility. His last contribution to the canon was the book of Revelation, where he describes himself as "your brother and companion in the tribulation and kingdom and patience of Jesus Christ." Even though he was the last remaining apostle and the patriarch of the church, we never find him lording it over anyone.

You may have a position that traditionally receives admiration or respect. It might be in your family, vocation, church, community, or some other arena. If you find yourself expecting a certain kind of treatment due to your position, think of John. Each time he climbed down from the pedestal others set him upon, respect for him shot higher.

PHILIPPIANS 3:10–11

[I count all things loss] that I may know Him and the power of His resurrection, and the fellowship of His sufferings, being conformed to His death, if, by any means, I may attain to the resurrection from the dead.

In his early years, John had a thirst for glory and an aversion to suffering. His thirst for glory is seen in his desire for the chief throne. His aversion to suffering is seen in the fact that he and the other apostles abandoned Jesus and fled on the night of His arrest. Both desires are understandable. But if we desire to participate in heavenly glory, we must also be willing to partake of earthly sufferings.

When you encounter severe difficulties—if you haven't already, you soon will!—a natural response is to find a way to end suffering as quickly as possible by any available means. Let me encourage you to do something supernatural. Ask God to sanctify your trial by using that difficult circumstance to help you identify with Christ and to increase your knowledge of Him. Then allow your pain to keep you in prayer. You may be surprised to discover how richly God can bless you in the midst of your trials.

They said to Him, "Grant us that we may sit, one on Your right hand and the other on Your left, in Your glory." But Jesus said to them, "You do not know what you ask. Are you able to drink the cup that I drink, and be baptized with the baptism that I am baptized with?" They said to Him, "We are able."

Suffering is both the price of glory and the prelude to glory. Therefore, our suffering as believers is the assurance of the glory that is yet to come. All the disciples needed to learn this. They *all* wanted the chief seats in glory, but Jesus said there is a price for those seats. Not only are they reserved for the humble, but those who sit in them will first be prepared for the place of honor by learning humility that can come only by enduring affliction. That's the essence of Jesus' warning to John and his brother.

How eagerly and how naively the ambitious Sons of Thunder assured the Lord that they would be able to drink the cup He would drink and be baptized with His suffering! When their Master's ordeal began, they fled into the night. Thankfully for all of us, Christ does not regard such failures as final.

PHILIPPIANS 3:10–11

[I also count all things loss] that I may know Him and the power of His resurrection, and the fellowship of His sufferings, being conformed to His death, if, by any means, I may attain to the resurrection from the dead.

On the night of Jesus' arrest, John probably began to understand the bitterness of the cup he would have to drink. We know from his account of Jesus' trial that he and Peter followed Jesus to the house of the high priest (John 18:15). There he watched as Jesus was bound and beaten. He was standing close enough to the cross for Jesus to see him (19:16) and probably watched as the Roman soldiers drove in the nails. And perhaps as he watched he realized then and there how awful the cup was he had so hastily volunteered to drink!

You may never be martyred for your trust in Christ, and it is even less likely that you will literally be crucified. However, suffering is assured for all who are truly faithful (2 Timothy 3:12). Choose now how you will respond. Choose to drink deeply from Christ's cup by facing difficulties with the same dignity He did. Then you will "know Him and the power of His resurrection, and the fellowship of His sufferings."

MARK 14:50

Then they all forsook Him and fled.

On the night of Jesus' arrest, all eleven disciples cowered for an unknown period of time before two, Peter and John, emerged to discover what lay ahead for Jesus. Every disciple failed—and failed badly—that night. Thankfully, all of them except Judas, the betrayer, was forgiven and reclaimed by the Lord for His service. Moreover, every one of them ultimately learned to suffer willingly for Christ's sake. In fact, most of them gave their lives as martyrs. Only John lived to old age. But even so, he suffered. He was still enduring earthly anguish and persecution long after the others were already in glory.

On occasion, believers have the opportunity to sacrifice their lives in one grand gesture, allowing their deaths to be a dramatic witness to the power of Jesus Christ. More often, however, we are given the opportunity to sacrifice our lives one day at a time, the impact of which is no less dramatic or profound. Begin by sacrificing this day of your life.

ROMANS 8:37–39

Yet in all these things we are more than conquerors through Him who loved us. For I am persuaded that neither death nor life, nor angels nor principalities nor powers, nor things present nor things to come, nor height nor depth, nor any other created thing, shall be able to separate us from the love of God which is in Christ Jesus our Lord.

When John's brother James became the church's first martyr, John bore the loss in a more personal way than the others. As each of the other disciples was martyred one by one, John suffered the grief and pain of additional loss. These were his friends and companions. Soon he alone was left. In some ways, that may have been the most painful suffering of all.

Interestingly, when John penned his account of Jesus' life, long after evil, corrupt men killed his companions, he called himself "the disciple whom Jesus loved." During times of loss, our flesh would have us believe that God has forsaken us, yet John felt the love of Christ more keenly as the years passed. This convinces me that John made a deliberate, daily choice to see the love of Christ in his suffering. Therefore, let us choose likewise. When the next difficulty comes your way, choose to see the world's evil wrapped in the love of Christ.

I, John, both your brother and companion in the tribulation and kingdom and patience of Jesus Christ, was on the island that is called Patmos for the word of God and for the testimony of Jesus Christ.

It is very likely that John eventually became the pastor of the church founded in Ephesus by the apostle Paul. From there, during a great persecution of the church under the Roman Emperor Domitian, John was banished to a prison community on Patmos, a small island off the west coast of modern Turkey.

Patmos is still a rugged, harsh place to live, even today. It would have been many times more difficult for an aged man in ancient times, made to struggle for the most basic necessities of life, cut off from those he loved, and treated with cruelty. But he learned to bear suffering willingly, choosing to keep the words *tribulation* and *patience* closely linked as he received and recorded the apocalyptic visions described in the book of Revelation.

Reasonable people take reasonable action to find relief from suffering whenever they can. There is no sin in that. However, some tribulations leave us only one response. We must endure with patience. Beware trying so hard to escape your pain that you miss the sanctifying benefit of it.

But also for this very reason, giving all diligence, add to your faith virtue, to virtue knowledge, to knowledge self-control, to self-control perseverance, to perseverance godliness, to godliness brotherly kindness, and to brotherly kindness love.

John bore his sufferings willingly. There is no complaint about his hardship anywhere in his epistles or the book of Revelation. He always spoke of patience in the same breath he mentioned tribulation. He was looking forward calmly to the day when he would partake in the promised glory of the kingdom. Yet he continued to serve the Lord and His church with diligent resolve.

What a marvelously balanced approach to life in both joy and sorrow. The mature believer accepts earthly joy as a foretaste of heavenly glory and looks beyond temporal suffering to anticipate eternity in the presence of Christ. However, no one ever said this would be easy. Unfortunately, the only way to master this balance is to endure suffering.

When difficulties inevitably strike, that is your signal that class is in session.

JOHN 19:26–27

When Jesus therefore saw His mother, and the disciple whom He loved
standing by, He said to His mother, "Woman, behold your son!" Then He
said to the disciple, "Behold your mother!" And from that hour that disciple
took her to his own home.

By the end of Christ's earthly ministry, John learned his lessons well. Powerful evidence of this is seen in a vignette from the cross. As Jesus approached death, He looked down from the cross and entrusted the care of His mother, Mary, to the once brash and unstable John. Obviously, he had learned to be a humble, loving servant. Several witnesses in early church history record that John never left Jerusalem or the care of Mary until she died.

The power of the gospel never fails to surprise and amaze me. My confidence in the transforming effect of grace has been challenged at times but has nevertheless grown stronger as men and women turn from lives of depraved indifference to conscientious commitment to the call of Christ.

Can the same be said of you? John was never perfect and neither will you ever be. But can you share with someone a "then vs. now" story that would convince him or her that the grace of God is real?

But as for you, speak the things which are proper for sound doctrine: that the older men be sober, reverent, temperate, sound in faith, in love, in patience; the older women likewise, that they be reverent in behavior, not slanderers, not given to much wine, teachers of good things.

John reminds me of many seminary graduates whom I have known, including myself as a younger man. I recall when I came out of seminary, I was loaded to the gills with truth but somewhat short on patience. I had a strong temptation to come blasting into the church, dump the truth on everyone, and expect an immediate response. I needed to learn patience, tolerance, mercy, grace, forgiveness, tenderness, compassion—all the characteristics of love. It is wonderful to be bold and thunderous, but love is necessary balance. John is a superb model for such young men and women.

1 PETER 4:8

Above all things have fervent love for one another, for "love will cover a multitude of sins."

It may seem amazing that Jesus loved a man who wanted to burn up a whole town of Samaritans. He loved a man who was obsessed with status and position. He loved a man who abandoned Him and fled rather than suffer for His sake. But in loving John, Jesus transformed him into a radically different person—a man who modeled the same kind of love Jesus had shown him.

The Greek term translated "fervent" was an adjective used to describe the taut, straining muscles of an athlete as he strove for victory. The love of Jesus for His disciples brought Him to the point of death and beyond. His love not only redeemed them from slavery to sin; it transformed them completely. If you have received the saving, transforming love of Christ, you are invited to share that powerful love with others. Someone nearby needs what you have been equipped to supply.

1 PETER 1:22-23

Since you have purified your souls in obeying the truth through the Spirit in sincere love of the brethren, love one another fervently with a pure heart, having been born again, not of corruptible seed but incorruptible, through the word of God which lives and abides forever.

John used the word *truth* some forty-five times in his gospel and epistles. But it is interesting that he also used the world *love* more than eighty times. Clearly, he learned the balance Christ taught him. He learned to love others as the Lord had loved Him. Love became the anchor and centerpiece of the truth he was most concerned with.

One of the lessons of John's life and experience is that love and truth are never at odds with one another. They are always in perfect harmony, even though in our fallenness we struggle to maintain the balance. The depraved human heart distrusts truth and will remain steadfastly closed for fear of destruction. Love, however, softens the hardened heart. Love and truth should therefore never be divorced.

That's why we are commanded always to speak the truth in love. Don't pretend you are showing love if you deliberately withhold hard truth from someone who is walking in darkness; and don't imagine that you are a defender of God's truth if you lack His love.

JOHN 15:9

"As the Father loved Me, I also have loved you; abide in My love."

John's theology is best described as a theology of love. He taught that God is a God of love, that God loved His own Son, that God loved the world, that God is loved by Christ, that Christ loved His disciples, that Christ's disciples loved Him, that all people should love Christ, that we should love one another, and that love fulfills the law. Love was a critical part of every element of John's teaching. It was the dominant theme of his entire ministry.

This love is not mere sentiment. Godly, Christlike love seeks the good of the other above all else, including one's own desires. Imagine a community in which genuine love permeated every member. Imagine how utterly content and fulfilled each person would be without any need for selfish thinking, self-centered motives, or self-fulfilling choices.

If John's theology is to become a practical reality, someone must be the first to act. Are you willing to lead the way?

3 JOHN 9–10

I wrote to the church, but Diotrephes, who loves to have the preeminence among them, does not receive us. Therefore, if I come, I will call to mind his deeds which he does, prating against us with malicious words. And not content with that, he himself does not receive the brethren, and forbids those who wish to, putting them out of the church.

John's love never slid into indulgent sentimentality. To the very end of his life John was still a thunderous defender of the truth. He lost none of his intolerance for lies. In his epistles, written near the end of his life, he was still waging spiritual warfare against errant Christologies, against anti-Christian deception, against sin, and against immorality. He was in that sense a Son of Thunder to the end. I think the Lord knew that the most powerful advocate of love needed to be a man who never compromised the truth.

That is the nature of biblical love. It "does not rejoice in iniquity, but rejoices in the truth" (1 Corinthians 13:6). Of course, the worldly concept of "love" is nothing like that. How does your own understanding of love measure up?

That which was from the beginning, which we have heard, which we have seen with our eyes, which we have looked upon, and our hands have handled, concerning the Word of life—the life was manifested, and we have seen, and bear witness, and declare to you that eternal life which was with the Father and was manifested to us—that which we have seen and heard we declare to you, that you also may have fellowship with us; and truly our fellowship is with the Father and with His Son Jesus Christ.

Another favorite word of John's was *witness*. He used it nearly seventy times. He refers to the witness of John the Baptist, the witness of Scripture, the witness of the Father, the witness of Christ, the witness of miracles, the witness of the Holy Spirit, and the witness of the apostles. In each case, these were witnesses to the *truth*.

The Greek word for witness is *marturia*, from which we derive our word "martyr." As the last living apostle, John had seen a lot of witnessing, especially in the extreme sense of giving one's life as a testimony of Jesus Christ. And this undoubtedly encouraged his passionate dedication to truth.

As you review your spiritual journey, you will likely find several witnesses to the truth who influenced, encouraged, challenged, and confirmed you along the way. Take time now to thank God for their impact and, if possible, express your appreciation to them—preferably in writing.

JOHN 13:34-35

"A new commandment I give to you, that you love one another; as I have loved you, that you also love one another. By this all will know that you are My disciples, if you have love for one another."

John died, by most accounts, around AD 98, during the reign of Emperor Trajan. Jerome says in his commentary on Galatians that the aged apostle John was so frail in his final days at Ephesus that he had to be carried into the church. One phrase was constantly on his lips: "My little children, love one another." Asked why he always said this, he replied, "It is the Lord's command, and if this alone be done, it is enough."

Indeed, if we focused on just this one expression of the Christian life, nearly everything else would fall into place. Let me challenge you to make this day one in which you intentionally focus all of your thoughts on loving those around you—not merely seeking warm feelings, but expressing love in tangible acts of kindness.

For when we were still without strength, in due time Christ died for the ungodly.

Ruth's life is a perfect depiction of the story of redemption, told with living, breathing symbols. Ruth herself furnishes a fitting picture of every sinner. While the life of Rahab pictures the ugliness of sin, the life of Ruth depicts the helplessness of sinners. In strictly human terms, she was quite admirable, but she was nonetheless unable to redeem herself by *any* means. Tragic circumstances reduced her to abject poverty; outcast, exiled, and totally bereft of resources. She was a widow and a foreigner who went to live in a strange land.

The Rahabs of the world have less trouble recognizing their need for a savior than the Ruths, who lead respectable lives and for whom life is relatively easy. It's not until evil strips them of their comforts and leaves them helpless do they realize that they too need rescuing—not only from the world's evil, but from their own sin as well.

Now it came to pass, in the days when the judges ruled, that there was a famine in the land. And a certain man of Bethlehem, Judah, went to dwell in the country of Moab, he and his wife [Naomi] and his two sons.

Ruth's story began near the end of the era of the Judges in the Old Testament, about a century before David, in an age characterized by anarchy, confusion, and unfaithfulness to the law of God. While living in Moab, the two sons married local women—Orpah and Ruth—despite the fact that Moabite culture practically epitomized everything faithful Israelites were supposed to shun. Most faithful Israelites would not have approved of the marriages. Nevertheless, Naomi, seems to have graciously accepted her daughters-in-law.

Before long, all three men died, leaving their wives to fend for themselves, which in that culture was nearly an impossible situation. Three widows, with no children and no responsible relatives, in a time of famine could not hope to survive for long. While Orpah returned to her family, Ruth was determined to accompany Naomi on her journey home. Above all, her devotion to the God of Israel was real. The witness of Naomi and her family must have made a powerful impression on Ruth.

But Ruth said: "Entreat me not to leave you, or to turn back from following after you; for wherever you go, I will go; and wherever you lodge, I will lodge; your people shall be my people, and your God, my God."

In agreeing to return to Bethlehem with Naomi, Ruth was agreeing to help support the aging woman. Because she was still quite young and physically strong, Ruth went to work in the fields, gleaning what the harvesters left behind in order to eke out an existence. (Gleaning was essentially Israel's public assistance program for the poor.) Ruth's options were limited to that, and that alone. No one else would provide for her as she had no relatives other than her mother-in-law. She was struggling to do what was right in a world dominated by famine, disease, and death, yet barely surviving. It seemed the Lord was distant.

Do you ever feel like God is far away, leaving you to survive on your own? Let me assure you, if you are united with Christ by faith, He is present with you (Hebrews 13:5), He loves you deeply, He is attending every circumstance, and while He is not the instigator of evil, He will use even life's setbacks to your advantage. Continue to do what is right, and trust Him.

[Ruth] left, and went and gleaned in the field after the reapers. And she happened to come to the part of the field belonging to Boaz, who was of the family of Elimelech.

The language of the text suggests that Ruth gleaned in one of Boaz's fields purely by happenstance, which is a clever ploy on the part of the storyteller. With tongue in cheek, he will allow the tale to reveal the fact that nothing happens by "chance," but God is always behind the scenes, working all things together for the good of His people, those who love Him (Romans 8:28). While Ruth focused on making the best of her situation, the Lord was doing the same on her behalf.

Satan would love for you to give up right now. He would delight to hear you say, "Doing what is right has done me no good, so I may as well do what I please!" Don't let him succeed. Remain steadfastly, doggedly determined to continue doing what you know to be right and trust that God is working to multiply the good you do.

RUTH 2:11–12

Boaz . . . said to her, "It has been fully reported to me, all that you have done for your mother-in-law since the death of your husband, and how you have left your father and your mother and the land of your birth, and have come to a people whom you did not know before. The LORD repay your work, and a full reward be given you by the LORD God of Israel, under whose wings you have come for refuge."

Boaz visited his fields that very day, and when he noticed Ruth, he sought out the foreman of his crew and inquired about her. The foreman related to Boaz the complete story of Ruth's extraordinary faithfulness and commended her strong work ethic. Boaz immediately began to show her special favor, encouraging her to glean in his fields exclusively and to drink freely of his water. He even instructed the reapers to deliberately drop extra grain behind them for her to glean. The Lord impressed upon one faithful person to be an encouragement to another.

Boaz's grace and silent encouragements to Ruth are a living picture of the grace of Christ to His beloved ones. We may not always see clearly the many ways He makes sure our needs are met. But He manifests His kindness toward us behind the scenes in countless ways we may never even discern. That's why we are commanded to give thanks "in everything" (1 Thessalonians 5:18). Evidence of His providential care for us is everywhere for those who have eyes to see.

RUTH 2:20

Then Naomi said to her daughter-in-law, "Blessed be he of the LORD, who has not forsaken His kindness to the living and the dead!" And Naomi said to her, "This man is a relation of ours, one of our close relatives."

Ruth, as a foreigner, didn't understand the cultural implications of her "chance" meeting. But when she told Naomi the man who had been her benefactor was named Boaz, Naomi instantly saw the hand of God in the blessing. The Hebrew word translated "one of our close relatives" is *goel*. It is a technical term that means much more than "kinsman." The word *goel* includes the idea of redemption or deliverance. This was usually a prominent male in one's extended family, an official guardian of the family's honor. In the absence of government, he would avenge the blood of a murdered relative, buy back family lands sold under duress, pay the redemption price of one sold into slavery, or (if he were eligible for marriage) he could revive the family lineage when someone died without an heir.

Very often, we are unaware of the blessings that come our way. In fact, they might be staring us in the face. Sometimes we need a loved one to help us see.

ROMANS 5:8

God demonstrates His own love toward us, in that while we were still sinners, Christ died for us.

Naomi saw it as her duty as a mother-in-law to seek long-term security for this faithful Moabite girl who had so graciously proven her loyalty, generosity, diligence and strength of character throughout the hot and difficult harvest season. And the very moment she learned it was Boaz who had taken an interest in Ruth, she grasped the potential of her daughter-in-law's glad turn of events. He was not only a kinsman; he had the means to be a redeemer too.

There was a significant redemptive aspect to the function of a *goel*. Every kinsman-redeemer was, in effect, a living illustration of the position and work of Christ with respect to His people: He is our true Kinsman-Redeemer, who becomes our human Brother, buys us back from our bondage to evil, redeems our lives from death, and ultimately returns to us everything we lost because of sin—not only our own sin, but also the sin of the world against us. God has not left us alone to fend for ourselves, even though we deserve nothing.

PROVERBS 29:23

A man's pride will bring him low,
But the humble in spirit will retain honor.

If Boaz had ever been married, Scripture does not mention it. According to Jewish tradition, he was a lifelong bachelor. He may have had some physical imperfection or personality quirk that stood in the way of a suitable marriage arrangement. At the very least, he desperately needed prodding. Although he obviously took a keen interest in Ruth from the moment he first saw her, it does not seem to have entered his mind to pursue the *goel's* role on her behalf. By his own testimony, he was surprised that Ruth didn't deem him unsuitable for marriage.

Humble people often need prompting before they will engage their talents, or wield their influence, or draw upon their personal resources. They simply don't think of themselves as any different from anyone else. It's a wonderful quality, if not a little frustrating. So you might have to remind such a person that he or she is in a unique position to act.

RUTH 3:3–4

[Naomi said,] "Therefore wash yourself and anoint yourself, put on your best garment and go down to the threshing floor; but do not make yourself known to the man until he has finished eating and drinking. Then it shall be, when he lies down, that you shall notice the place where he lies; and you shall go in, uncover his feet, and lie down; and he will tell you what you should do."

What Naomi advised Ruth to do was shockingly forward. Her plan, in essence, was for Ruth to propose marriage to Boaz! By the custom of the time, following Naomi's instructions would indicate Ruth's willingness to marry Boaz without his first proposing.

The threshing floor was a site, most likely on a hill, where grain was tossed into the air in a breeze so that the light husks of chaff would be blown away. Boaz would work late, sleep outdoors, then arise early and go back to threshing. In accordance with Naomi's instructions, Ruth "came softly, uncovered his feet, and lay down" (3:7). It's unlikely that Ruth understood what was going on. She didn't know the people, Hebrew customs were a mystery to her, and Naomi didn't tell her what to expect. She followed instructions to the letter as an expression of her trust.

That kind of implicit obedience is the essence of true faith. How does your faith measure up?

RUTH 3:12–13

[Boaz said,] "Now it is true that I am a close relative; however, there is a relative closer than I. Stay this night, and in the morning it shall be that if he will perform the duty of a close relative for you—good; let him do it. But if he does not want to perform the duty for you, then I will perform the duty for you, as the LORD lives! Lie down until morning."

Ruth's proposal came as an overwhelming and unexpected blessing to Boaz, but he immediately knew that custom required him to defer to another relative who had first right of refusal. He swore his willingness to be her *goel* if possible and urged her to remain at his feet through the night. Being protective of Ruth's virtue, he woke her and sent her home just before dawn, but not before giving her a generous portion of grain as a gift for Naomi.

Boaz was a wise man of integrity, through and through. He could have taken advantage of the situation, but he determined to do everything in its proper order and in accordance with the customs of his community—rare behavior during the age of the Judges. His decision to set aside his own strong desires for the sake of doing things the right way makes Boaz a towering hero of faith. And what a perfect match he found in Ruth!

Then [Naomi] said, "Sit still, my daughter, until you know how the matter will turn out; for the man will not rest until he has concluded the matter this day."

Naomi had been around long enough to know a man of integrity when she saw one. And she was right about Boaz. He went immediately to the city gate and found Naomi's true next of kin. The two of them sat down in the presence of ten city elders and negotiated for the right to be Ruth's *goel*. That role involved, first of all, the buy-back of the property once owned by Naomi's dead husband. However, because of the intricacies of Hebrew custom, redeeming the land would not be lucrative unless the redeemer also married Ruth. Fortunately for Boaz and Ruth, the other relative was unable or unwilling to do this. He therefore relinquished his right.

Boaz was fair yet shrewd in his negotiations. Integrity doesn't require a person to become passive or weak, and it certainly doesn't demand one to accept the short end of a deal. It merely means that every word and deed is undergirded with truth.

RUTH 4:11

*And all the people who were at the gate, and the elders, said, "We are
witnesses. The LORD make the woman who is coming to your house like
Rachel and Leah, the two who built the house of Israel; and may you
prosper in Ephrathah and be famous in Bethlehem."*

Everyone loves a good love story, and the people of Bethlehem
were no exception. As word got out about the unusual transaction taking place in the city gate, the inhabitants of the city began to
congregate. They pronounced a blessing upon Boaz and his bride-to-be. And the blessing proved to be prophetic. Boaz and Ruth were
married, and the Lord soon blessed them with a son. They named
him Obed, who became the father of Jesse, the father of David. In
other words, Ruth was David's great-grandmother.

Ruth is a fitting symbol of every believer, and even of the
church itself—redeemed, brought into a position of great favor,
endowed with riches and privilege, exalted to be the Redeemer's
own bride, and loved by Him with the profoundest affection. That
is why the extraordinary story of her redemption ought to make
every true believer's heart resonate with gladness and thanksgiving for the One who, likewise, has redeemed us from our sin.

JOHN 1:43

The following day Jesus wanted to go to Galilee, and He found Philip and said to him, "Follow Me."

Philip is a Greek name meaning "lover of horses." He must also have had a Jewish name, because all twelve disciples were Jewish. But his Jewish name is never given. Greek civilization had spread through the Mediterranean world after the conquests of Alexander the Great, and many people in the Middle East had adopted Greek language, culture, and custom as their own. Perhaps Philip came from a family of these "Hellenistic" Jews, which means his addition only further diversified the group of disciples. To Simon, "the Zealot," and Matthew, the Roman collaborator, Jesus added a Jew whose family straddled the cultural fence.

It's a reminder that Christ redeems all kinds of sinners. Heaven will be populated with disciples called "out of every tribe and tongue and people and nation" (Revelation 5:9), as well as every class and cultural background—all of them made saints by the grace of God.

Now Philip was from Bethsaida, the city of Andrew and Peter.

The apostle Philip undoubtedly knew Peter, Andrew, James, and John. Because they were all God-fearing Jews, they probably grew up attending the same synagogue in Capernaum. And there is good biblical evidence that Philip, Nathanael, and Thomas were all fishermen from Galilee (John 21). Therefore, the innermost seven disciples were most likely friends, coworkers, colleagues, and rivals a long time before they followed Christ. However, Jesus found them at different times, in different places, and by a variety of means before officially calling them to follow.

One by one, each found the Messiah—or rather, was found by Him. The wisdom of God's plan is seen in Jesus' choice of these men to be His primary ambassadors in the expansion of the gospel. Collectively, they might seem unlikely candidates for such a high calling. You can bet no worldly entrepreneur or political strategist would select men like these for a task like that. But they were Christ's choice—and the *perfect* choice, "to put to shame the wise, and . . . to put to shame the things which are mighty" (1 Corinthians 1:27).

MATTHEW 10:1

And when He had called His twelve disciples to Him, He gave them power over unclean spirits, to cast them out, and to heal all kinds of sickness and all kinds of disease.

If seven of the twelve disciples were professional fishermen from the same small village long before they followed Christ, they undoubtedly formed a close-knit group as disciples. In a sense, this is somewhat surprising. We might have expected Jesus to take a different approach in choosing the Twelve. After all, He was appointing them to the formidable task of being apostles, proxies for Him after He departed the earth, men with full power of attorney to speak on His behalf. You might think He would scour the whole earth to find the most gifted and qualified men. But instead, He singled out a small group of fishermen, a diverse yet common group of individuals with unexceptional talents. And He said, "They will do."

Perhaps it can be said that Jesus would rather craft His own vessels than shop the world for the handiwork of another.

MATTHEW 10:24–25

"A disciple is not above his teacher, nor a servant above his master. It is enough for a disciple that he be like his teacher, and a servant like his master."

When assembling His core group of leader trainees, Jesus didn't look for the best and brightest in Israel. All He really required of them was availability. He would draw them to Himself, train them, gift them, and empower them to serve Him. Because they would preach Jesus' message and do miracles by His power, these rugged fishermen, tax collectors, zealots, and tradesmen were better suited to the task than a group of glittering prodigies trying to operate on their own talent might have been. After all, even these men behaved like prima donnas at times.

Unfortunately, many churches don't follow Jesus' model. When looking for leaders in their midst, they are more often impressed by professional achievement, financial success, business savvy, and political polish—none of which qualifies a man for spiritual leadership. How Christlike our churches would be if, instead, we looked to men who are perpetually available to the transforming work of Christ in their hearts.

MARK 4:22–23

"For there is nothing hidden which will not be revealed, nor has anything been kept secret but that it should come to light. If anyone has ears to hear, let him hear."

Nearly everything we know about Philip comes from John's gospel, in which we discover that Philip was a completely different kind of person from Peter, Andrew, James, or John. He is usually paired with Nathanael (also known as Bartholomew), so we can assume the two of them were close comrades. But Philip is singularly different from even his closest companion. In fact, he is unique among all the disciples.

Perhaps you often find yourself the "odd person out" in your community. Not shunned or ignored, necessarily, but feeling detached because you frequently view things from a unique perspective. If so, you are a great gift to your congregation! We're not supposed to be cookie-cutter saints, all exactly alike. God has gifted each of us differently for a reason: "The body is not one member but many. . . . If the whole body were an eye, where would be the hearing?" (1 Corinthians 12:14–17). Philip reminds us that the very things that make us different are often what make us most useful.

MATTHEW 17:19–20

Then the disciples came to Jesus privately and said, "Why could we not cast [the demon] out?" So Jesus said to them, "Because of your unbelief; for assuredly, I say to you, if you have faith as a mustard seed, you will say to this mountain, 'Move from here to there,' and it will move; and nothing will be impossible for you."

Piecing together all that the apostle John records about him, it seems Philip was a classic "process person." He was a facts-and-figures guy—a by-the-book, practical-minded, non-forward-thinking type of individual. He was the kind who tends to be a corporate killjoy, pessimistic, narrowly focused, sometimes missing the big picture, often obsessed with identifying reasons things *can't* be done rather than finding ways to do them. He was predisposed to be a pragmatist and a cynic—and sometimes a defeatist—rather than a visionary.

"Bean counters" can be both a blessing and a curse to visionary leaders. Their detail-oriented talents can either make possibilities impossible or bring dreams into sharper focus. It all depends upon whether their faith is real.

JOHN 1:43

The following day Jesus wanted to go to Galilee, and He found Philip and said to him, "Follow Me."

We first meet Philip in John 1, the day after Andrew, John, and Peter first encountered Jesus. Apparently Philip had also been a follower of the Baptizer. While Andrew and John had been directed to the Messiah by John the Baptist, this is the first time we read that Jesus Himself actually sought and found a particular disciple. This is not to say He didn't sovereignly seek and call the rest; however, the language describing Philip's calling is unique. He is the first one whom Jesus physically sought out and the first one to whom Jesus actually said, "Follow Me."

It's good to be submitted to the will of Christ and to be used by Him, but have you considered that you are *wanted* by the Lord simply because He desires to have you in His presence? Christ doesn't call disciples because He needs them; He called you because He loves you. And He went to great lengths to have you close to Him!

And another also said, "Lord, I will follow You, but let me first go and bid them farewell who are at my house." But Jesus said to him, "No one, having put his hand to the plow, and looking back, is fit for the kingdom of God."

It is interesting to note that at the end of His earthly ministry, Jesus had to say, "Follow Me," to Peter (John 21:19, 22). Peter apparently still needed that encouragement after his failure on the night of Jesus' betrayal. But Philip was the first to hear and obey those words. From the outset, Jesus actively sought his most careful disciple. And He found in Philip an eager and willing follower. It is obvious that Philip always had a seeking heart.

Although Jesus had only to call Philip once, we must not assume the disciple followed perfectly or even steadfastly. He didn't. Like the others, he fled when Jesus was arrested. Nevertheless, his discipleship was more careful than that of passionate Peter or the thunderous sons of Zebedee. He undoubtedly calculated the cost of discipleship early and then followed without ever looking back.

Discipleship is not an easy calling. Count the cost and then commit with a whole heart.

JAMES 4:6

But He gives more grace. Therefore He says: "God resists the proud, but gives grace to the humble."

While it is obvious Philip had a seeking heart, a seeking heart is always evidence that God is sovereignly drawing the person. Jesus said, "No one can come to Me unless the Father who sent Me draws him" (John 6:44); and again, "No one can come to Me unless it has been granted to him by My Father" (v. 65). So it was with Philip; so it is today.

Beware the temptation to look down on those who have not responded to the invitation, "Follow Me." You are no better than they. If you are a disciple, it is because of God's goodness and not your own. Therefore, make today a day of thanksgiving and praise for the grace you have been given by God. And may your thanksgiving produce in you a humble heart.

For indeed the gospel was preached to us as well as to them; but the word which they heard did not profit them, not being mixed with faith in those who heard it.

Obviously, Philip and Nathanael, like the first four disciples, had been studying the Law and the Prophets and were seeking the Messiah. That is why they had all gone to the wilderness to hear John the Baptist in the first place. So when Jesus came to Philip and said, "Follow Me," his ears, his eyes, and his heart were already open, and he was prepared to follow.

Philip's call is a perfect illustration of how both sovereign election and human choice exist in perfect harmony. The Lord found Philip, but Philip felt he had found the Lord. From a human perspective, both are true. Nevertheless, God's choice is determinant—always.

As you share the good news, share freely and with all, but be on the lookout for open ears, eyes, and hearts, for there you will find the sovereign plans of God ready to be fulfilled. And you just might be the foreordained means of accomplishing them!

JOHN 1:45

Philip found Nathanael and said to him, "We have found Him of whom Moses in the law, and also the prophets, wrote—Jesus of Nazareth, the son of Joseph."

From a human perspective—from Philip's point of view— meeting Jesus was the end of his search. By God's grace, he had been a faithful and true seeker. He was devoted to the Word of God, and he believed the Old Testament promise of a Messiah. Now he had found Him—or rather Philip had been found. And his first response upon meeting Jesus was to find his friend Nathanael, whom he knew to be searching as well, and to tell him about finding the Messiah.

God calls us to join Him in fulfilling His redemptive plan, not for His benefit but for ours. He wants us to share His joy in seeking and saving the lost. Right now, there are Philips and Nathanaels being drawn to Christ. Do you know who they are? Are you sufficiently invested in the lives of unsaved people to tell them about the Savior?

JOHN 4:32–34

[Jesus] said to them, "I have food to eat of which you do not know."
Therefore the disciples said to one another, "Has anyone brought Him
anything to eat?" Jesus said to them, "My food is to do the will of Him who
sent Me, and to finish His work."

I am convinced that friendships provide the most fertile soil for evangelism. When the reality of Christ is introduced into a relationship of love and trust that has already been established, the effect is powerful. And it seems that invariably, when someone becomes a true follower of Christ, that person's first impulse is to find a friend and introduce that friend to Christ. Unfortunately, that early excitement frequently fades and a general attitude of apathy takes over. But it doesn't have to be that way.

If this has happened to you, let me encourage you to periodically involve yourself in a ministry that has evangelism as its primary focus or participate in an evangelism training program. These have a way of reviving that early excitement and rebuilding confidence in the power of the gospel. Do this, not out of duty or obligation, but to claim the joy God has ordained for you.

JOHN 1:46

And Nathanael said to him, "Can anything good come out of Nazareth?"
Philip said to him, "Come and see."

When Nathanael first heard about Jesus from Philip, he was nonplussed. But Philip remained undaunted: "Come and see." Philip apparently believed with little hesitation. In human terms, no one had brought Philip to Jesus. He was like Simeon, "waiting for the Consolation of Israel, and the Holy Spirit was upon him" (Luke 2:25). He knew the Old Testament promises. He was ready. He was expectant. His heart was prepared. And he received Jesus gladly, unhesitatingly, as Messiah. It mattered not to him what kind of one-horse town the Messiah had grown up in.

Genuine belief in Christ occurs when truth meets a ready heart. Not everyone is so ready to accept Jesus as He is. Most prefer a savior of their own liking. Therefore, don't be discouraged when people do not respond positively to the good news. Keep the door open for them to know more, remain sensitive to their readiness, and pray!

JOHN 6:37

"All that the Father gives Me will come to Me, and the one who comes to Me I will by no means cast out."

The ease with which Philip believed is remarkable, which was frankly out of character for the methodical disciple. The fact that he responded so readily reveals the great care the Lord took to prepare his heart. His natural tendency might have been to hold back, doubt, ask questions, and wait and see. He was not usually a very decisive person. But, thankfully, in this case, he was already being drawn to Christ by the Father. Therefore, we can say for certain, his response was quite supernatural.

When sharing the gospel with others, we can sometimes make the mistake of thinking that their believing depends upon our effectiveness. While I wholeheartedly encourage people to practice and prepare to be as effective as possible, I also remind them that "success" or "failure" is in God's hands. He didn't call us to be "successful"; He calls us to be faithful.

Then Jesus lifted up His eyes, and seeing a great multitude coming toward Him, He said to Philip, "Where shall we buy bread, that these may eat?"

The gospel of John describes how a great multitude had sought out Jesus and found Him on a mountainside with His disciples. There were five thousand men in the crowd and, undoubtedly, several more thousand women and children. As evening approached, the people needed to eat. Jesus turned to Philip and said, "Where shall we buy bread, that these may eat?" Why did He single Philip out and ask him? According to John, "to test him, for He Himself knew what He would do" (John 6:5–6).

The Lord frequently gives us impossible tasks, not to discourage or humiliate us, but to strengthen our faith muscle through exercise. He brings us to the brink of our own abilities and then beyond so that we will do what comes unnaturally to the flesh: trust Him.

The next time you face difficulties or challenges beyond your ability, remember, He already knows what He will do. This is your opportunity to trust Him.

JOHN 6:6

But this [Jesus] said to test [Philip], for He Himself knew what He would do.

P hilip was apparently the apostolic administrator—the bean counter. It is likely that he was charged with arranging meals and logistics. We know that Judas was in charge of keeping the money, so it makes sense that someone else was also charged with coordinating the acquisition and distribution of meals and supplies. It was a task that certainly suited Philip's personality. He was the type of person who in every meeting says, "I don't think we can do that"— the master of the impossible.

I don't mean to suggest we should be irresponsible; however, sometimes the path forward is very clear and the only obstacle is a shortfall of one kind or another. In those cases, we must see with supernatural eyes and trust God to provide. He never leads us to accomplish anything without supplying the means.

IMPOSSIBLE, NATURALLY

1 CORINTHIANS 2:14–15

But the natural man does not receive the things of the Spirit of God, for they are foolishness to him; nor can he know them, because they are spiritually discerned. But he who is spiritual judges all things, yet he himself is rightly judged by no one.

Philip was quick to answer Jesus when challenged to feed the multitude. He had apparently been thinking through the difficulties of food supply from the moment he first saw the crowd. Instead of thinking, *What a glorious occasion! Jesus is going to teach this crowd. What a tremendous opportunity for the Lord!*—all pessimistic Philip could see was a multitude of grumbling bellies. Jesus tested Philip, not to find out what he was thinking; Jesus already knew that. He wasn't asking for a plan; Jesus already had one. He was testing Philip so Philip would reveal to *himself* what he was like.

Sometimes the Lord has to bring us to the end of our own abilities in order to get our attention. Rather than banging your head against the wall of impossibility, why not ask the Lord for insight? Perhaps He wants the opportunity to teach you something new.

JOHN 14:12

"Most assuredly, I say to you, he who believes in Me, the works that I do he will do also; and greater works than these he will do, because I go to My Father."

Philip had been there when the Lord created wine out of water (John 2:2). He had already seen numerous times when Jesus had healed people, including several creative and regenerative miracles. But when he saw the great crowd, he began to feel overwhelmed by the impossible. He lapsed into materialistic thinking. And when Jesus tested his faith, he responded with open unbelief. *It can't be done.* His thoughts were pessimistic, analytical, and pragmatic—completely materialistic and earthbound.

When confronted by an overwhelming difficulty, we tend to rely on our natural abilities rather than trust the Lord, and the results are invariably panic and paralysis. The Lord must retrain our instincts to rely upon Him first. Fortunately, we can be proactive students. When you face your next big challenge, take a few moments to reflect on your natural response and ask the Lord to give you a new perspective, *His* perspective.

MARK 6:38–39

[Jesus] said to them, "How many loaves do you have? Go and see." And when they found out they said, "Five, and two fish." Then He commanded them to make them all sit down in groups on the green grass.

Philip was obsessed with mundane matters and therefore overwhelmed by the impossibility of the immediate problem. He should have said, "Lord, if You want to feed them, feed them. I'm just going to stand back and watch how You do it. I know You can, Lord. You made wine at Cana and fed Your children manna in the wilderness. Do it. We will tell everyone to get in line, and You just make the food."

How often we forget that our biggest problems are His greatest opportunities to demonstrate His power and grace!

What is your most difficult challenge today? Have you given it to God in prayer?

Now there were certain Greeks among those who came up to worship at the feast. Then they came to Philip, who was from Bethsaida of Galilee, and asked him, saying, "Sir, we wish to see Jesus."

These Greeks were either God-fearing Gentiles or full-fledged proselytes to Judaism who were coming to Jerusalem to worship God at the Passover. When they wanted an audience with Jesus, they approached Philip, perhaps because of his Greek name. It was not a difficult or complex request, yet Philip seems to have been unsure what to do with them.

Hopefully you will have many opportunities like Philip's. Do you know how you will respond? Introducing others to Christ isn't complicated, but it can feel that way if you aren't prepared. Let me encourage you to participate in an evangelism training program. It will give you valuable knowledge and skills, and it will help you build confidence.

JOHN 1:11–12

He came to His own, and His own did not receive Him. But as many as received Him, to them He gave the right to become children of God, to those who believe in His name.

Why did Philip seem to balk at introducing a group of Greek worshipers to Jesus? He may have been confused by a statement Jesus made earlier in His ministry. "I was not sent except to the lost sheep of the house of Israel" (Matthew 15:24). Was that principle meant to prohibit Gentiles from ever being introduced to Jesus? Of course not. Jesus was simply identifying the normal priority of His ministry: "to the Jew first and also to the Greek" (Romans 2:10). It was a general principle, not an iron-clad law. But some people don't appreciate general rules of thumb; they want every rule to be rigid and inviolable. Philip seems to have been a little like that.

When it comes to spiritual things, we must learn to think biblically. Personal feelings, long-standing traditions, cultural prejudices, and uncritical assumptions are not safe guides to truth in matters of faith. In this case, if Philip had truly understood the spirit of Christ, He would have known that the one who came to seek and save the lost would by no means cast out those who came to Him (John 6:37).

[The Greeks] came to Philip, who was from Bethsaida of Galilee, and asked him, saying, "Sir, we wish to see Jesus." Philip came and told Andrew, and in turn Andrew and Philip told Jesus.

While Philip preferred the safety of rigid rules, he had a good heart. However, Philip was not a decisive man. There was no precedent for introducing Gentiles to Jesus, so he enlisted Andrew's help before doing anything. Andrew would bring anyone to Jesus. Perhaps he did this so Andrew would get the blame if anyone objected.

Philip need not have worried. Jesus is not the kind of Master who broods about looking for an excuse to chastise His followers. He encouraged bold action and creative thinking. That was His whole purpose in challenging the disciples with the problem of feeding the multitude. Jesus said, in effect, "Think big. I'm God; I can do anything!"

You serve a God of infinite resources and limitless power. How does your vision of Christ and His kingdom reflect that?

"If anyone serves Me, let him follow Me; and where I am, there My servant will be also. If anyone serves Me, him My Father will honor."

When Jesus met the Greeks, He boldly declared Himself to be the fulfillment of Old Testament prophecies. He preached the gospel to them and invited them to become His disciples. Was it the right thing to bring those Greeks to Jesus? Absolutely. Jesus Himself welcomes all comers to drink freely of the water of life (Revelation 22:17). It would have been wrong to turn those people away. Philip seemed to know that in his heart, even if his head was obsessed with protocol and procedure.

Sometimes our hearts tug us in directions we know to be good and right, yet feel risky or implausible. Perhaps we doubt our ability or the idea feels awkwardly uncharacteristic. I have little doubt that the Holy Spirit is growing us beyond the confines of our former ways and we must risk feeling or looking foolish. So why not do as Philip did? Seek out a trusted friend to join you as you explore this new direction. And before doing anything else, take it to God in prayer.

JOHN 14:3–4

"And if I go and prepare a place for you, I will come again and receive you to Myself; that where I am, there you may be also. And where I go you know, and the way you know."

Jesus declared that He was going to prepare a place for His followers and promised to return to receive them to Himself. He then added, "And where I go you know, and the way you know" (John 14:4). Obviously, the *where* was heaven, and the *way* there was the way He had outlined in the gospel. But the disciples were slow to catch His meaning. Nevertheless, Jesus gave His followers words of hope to carry them through the difficult days to come.

Because we cannot see the future, we may expect our lives to unfold a certain way. But rarely do things go exactly as we plan. We simply cannot see the future or anticipate exactly how it will unfold. So we must ask, *In what do I trust? My plans or my God?* Furthermore, we must ask, *What is the best way ahead in the uncertainty of the future? My plans, or God's plan for me?*

Jesus didn't say, "I am the means of achieving *your* goals." He said, "I am the way, the truth, and the life. No one comes to the Father except through Me" (John 14:6).

JOHN 14:16–17

And I will pray the Father, and He will give you another Helper, that He may abide with you forever—the Spirit of truth, whom the world cannot receive, because it neither sees Him nor knows Him; but you know Him, for He dwells with you and will be in you.

On the eve of Jesus' betrayal and arrest, He gathered the Twelve for a final meal. Their formal training had officially come to an end. And yet their faith was still pathetically weak. Many of the most important lessons He had taught them appear to have gone unheeded. They were "foolish . . . and slow of heart to believe" (Luke 24:25). The disciples would have to endure three days of bewildered disillusionment. Then, they would have to wait another forty-seven days after His resurrection to receive God's Holy Spirit before they would fully comprehend the "where" and the "way" of Jesus' teaching.

I am grateful the Lord is so patient. I wish my flesh did not make me so insensitive to His teaching that He must allow the pain of life to make me receptive. But He is long-suffering and gentle—allowing no more affliction than is absolutely necessary to transform me into the likeness of His Son.

JOHN 14:7

"If you had known Me, you would have known My Father also; and from now on you know Him and have seen Him."

On the eve of His ordeal, Jesus made an explicit claim about His own deity. He was stating in the clearest possible language that He is God. Christ and His Father are of the same essence. To know Christ is to know the Father, because the different persons of the Trinity are one in their very essence. Jesus *is* God. To see Him is to see God. So when Philip spoke up and said, "Lord, show us the Father, and it is sufficient for us" (John 14:8), Jesus was profoundly sad. "Show us the Father?" What did he think Jesus had been doing? For three years Philip had gazed into the very face of God, but his earthbound thinking, his materialism, his skepticism, his obsession with mundane details, his preoccupation with business details, and his small-mindedness had shut him off from a full apprehension of whose presence he had enjoyed.

God became a man and has invited you to know Him personally. Perhaps you've been introduced already. Good. But do you *know* Him?

I CORINTHIANS 1:26–27

For you see your calling, brethren, that not many wise according to the flesh, not many mighty, not many noble, are called. But God has chosen the foolish things of the world to put to shame the wise, and God has chosen the weak things of the world to put to shame the things which are mighty.

Philip, like the other disciples, was a man of limited ability. He was a man of weak faith and imperfect understanding. Skeptical, analytical, pessimistic, reluctant, unsure. He wanted to go by the book all the time. Facts and figures filled his thoughts. He was sometimes unable to grasp the big picture of Christ's divine power, person, and grace. If we were interviewing Philip for the role to which Jesus called him, we might say, "He's out. You can't make him one of the twelve most important people in the history of the world." But Jesus said, "He's exactly what I'm looking for."

Thankfully, Jesus calls people like Philip—lots of them.

He called me. He called you. We can second-guess His judgment about our ability, or we can allow His power to be made perfect in our weakness. Each sunrise is a new call to submission. What will be your answer?

JOHN 6:5–6

Then Jesus lifted up His eyes, and seeing a great multitude coming toward Him, He said to Philip, "Where shall we buy bread, that these may eat?" But this He said to test him, for He Himself knew what He would do.

Tradition tells us that Philip was greatly used in the spread of the early church and was among the first of the apostles to suffer martyrdom. By most accounts he was put to death by stoning at Heliopolis, in Phrygia (Asia Minor), eight years after the martyrdom of James. Before his death, multitudes came to Christ under his preaching. He obviously overcame the natural tendencies of his earlier life that so often hampered his faith, and he stands with the other apostles as proof that "the things which are impossible with men are possible with God" (Luke 18:27).

I have little doubt that your life is surrounded by impossibilities and permeated with inadequacies. What life is not? As with Philip, the Lord isn't daunted by your incapacity. His challenge to you is a test, "for He Himself knows what He will do." All He wants from you is trust.

2 CORINTHIANS 12:9

[God] said to me, "My grace is sufficient for you, for My strength is made perfect in weakness."

Therefore most gladly I will rather boast in my infirmities, that the power of Christ may rest upon me.

Hannah's name means "grace." It's a fitting designation for a woman whose life was crowned with grace and who became a living emblem of the grace of motherhood. Yet Hannah almost despaired of ever *becoming* a mother. Like Sarah, she was childless and distraught over it yet ultimately received the blessing she sought from God. And like Sarah, the answers to her prayers turned out to be exceedingly and abundantly more significant than she had ever dared to ask or think.

While God chose to bless each woman by giving her the child she so desperately longed to bear, He does not always choose to grant His people's requests, even when those requests are honorable and good. Our God is not a genie who can be coaxed or tricked into granting wishes. He is our sovereign Lord who has a plan. And His love for us abounds even when we don't get the outcome we so desperately long for.

PSALM 127:4−5

Like arrows in the hand of a warrior,
So are the children of one's youth.
Happy is the man who has his quiver full of them;
They shall not be ashamed,
But shall speak with their enemies in the gate.

A study of Hannah's life reveals the classic profile of a godly mother. Her son, Samuel, was the last of the judges. He was also a priest—the one who formally inaugurated the true royal line of Israel by anointing David as king. Samuel became a towering figure in Israel's history. Thus Hannah's life often mirrored that of the original matriarch, Sarah. And the fruit of her motherhood stood as a testament to her amazing faith and perseverance.

While no parent should be judged by the success or failure of his or her children, we cannot ignore a parent's influence on a life. When children grow to become great men and women of God, we should look to the parents, thank them for their faith and perseverance, and learn by their examples.

By the way, have you thanked your mother or father lately?

Do not be envious of evil men,
Nor desire to be with them;
For their heart devises violence,
And their lips talk of troublemaking.

Hannah was an obscure woman living in a remote part of Israel with her husband, Elkanah, a son of the priestly tribe of Levi. Hannah faithfully traveled with her husband to the tabernacle each year to worship and offer a sacrifice. Scripture portrays them as a devout family living in a dismal period of Israel's history. The Bible reminds us that "the two sons of Eli, Hophni and Phinehas, the priests of the Lord," served in the tabernacle (1 Samuel 1:3). The sons of Eli were two of the most corrupt priests the nation had ever known.

This must have been especially difficult for Hannah to witness. It would appear that the Lord tolerated—even rewarded—unfaithful priests. Meanwhile, she could not bear children who might be worthier servants of God in His place of worship. Fortunately, her confusion and sorrow didn't turn into bitterness. Rather than turning away from worship, she turned toward God in humble surrender to His will and His way.

1 SAMUEL 1:5–6

To Hannah [Elkanah] would give a double portion, for he loved Hannah, although the LORD had closed her womb. And her rival also provoked her severely, to make her miserable, because the LORD had closed her womb.

In spite of her gracious character, Hannah's home life was often troubled and sorrowful. Her husband was a bigamist, and as usual this caused severe tension in the family. Peninnah—called Hannah's rival—deliberately provoked her, goading her about the fact that the Lord had withheld children from her. Elkanah preferred Hannah, whom he loved deeply, but that only magnified the bitter rivalry between the women. God, of course, designed marriage as a monogamous relationship, so it is no surprise to see bigamy causing such strife. But this was not in Hannah's power to change.

Godly people frequently find themselves in difficult circumstances they cannot change. While it appears that God is not blessing the faithful, we see only what is external and immediate. In reality, the difficulties of today are God's means of bringing great honor to those who love Him and trust in His goodness.

My son, hear the instruction of your father,
And do not forsake the law of your mother;
For they will be a graceful ornament on your head,
And chains about your neck.

Hannah was in constant anguish because of her own infertility. Becoming a mother was her one ambition in life, which I am convinced was no selfish aspiration. She understood that motherhood is the highest calling God can bestow on any woman. This is not to suggest, of course, that motherhood is the *only* role for women or even their primary reason for being. Nevertheless, this high calling manifests itself as an intense, natural longing in the hearts of most women.

The Bible's exaltation of motherhood is often scorned by our more "enlightened" age. In fact, in this generation, motherhood is frequently derided and belittled, but it has been God's plan from the beginning that women should train and nurture godly children and thus leave a powerful imprint on society through the home. Hannah is a classic illustration. Through her role as a mother, she would directly confront the evil of Eli's sons.

1 SAMUEL 1:11

Then [Hannah] made a vow and said, "O LORD of hosts, if You will indeed look on the affliction of Your maidservant and remember me, and not forget Your maidservant, but will give Your maidservant a male child, then I will give him to the LORD all the days of his life, and no razor shall come upon his head."

We first encounter Hannah when Israel was in desperate need of a great man, someone who would point God's covenant nation back toward Him. Hannah became the woman whom God used to help shape that man. Her son, Samuel, proved to be the one man who could fill the leadership void. His character bore the clear stamp of his mother's influence, even though he left home at such an early age.

Hannah is a reminder that mothers are the makers of men and women, and the architects of the next generation. Her earnest prayer for a child was the beginning of a series of events that helped turn back the spiritual darkness and backsliding in Israel. She set in motion a chain of events that would ultimately usher in a profound spiritual awakening at the dawn of the Davidic dynasty.

1 SAMUEL 1:8–9

Then Elkanah her husband said to her, "Hannah, why do you weep? Why do you not eat? And why is your heart grieved? Am I not better to you than ten sons?" So Hannah arose after they had finished eating and drinking in Shiloh.

I believe Hannah's influence as an extraordinary woman of God is traceable to the three great loves of her life. The first—though not the most important—was her love for her husband. Obviously, her marriage was not a perfect one, being marred by polygamous tensions, but it was solid. Her husband loved her with sincere affection, and he knew her love for him was returned.

Hannah's love for her husband is the first key to understanding her profound influence as a mother. Contrary to popular opinion, the most important characteristic of a godly mother is not her relationship with her *children*. It is with her *mate*. The same is true of a godly father. The love between a husband and wife is the real key to a thriving family. The marriage is the wellspring of the family; the love between the husband and wife produces children and then nurtures them.

Whenever the time came for Elkanah to make an offering, he would give portions to Peninnah his wife and to all her sons and daughters. But to Hannah he would give a double portion, for he loved Hannah, although the LORD had closed her womb.

The centrality of marriage was very evident between Elkanah and Hannah. With all their domestic issues, they nonetheless had a healthy marriage and an abiding love for one another. Their inability to have children together was like an open wound. But it was an experience that drew out of Elkanah tender expressions of love for his wife.

All parents need to heed this lesson: what you communicate to your children through your marital relationship will stay with them for the rest of their lives. By watching how mother and father relate to one another, they will learn the most fundamental lessons of life—love, self-sacrifice, integrity, virtue, sin, sympathy, compassion, understanding, and forgiveness. Futhermore, nothing gives children a greater sense of security and well-being than seeing Mom and Dad faithfully in love with each other.

1 SAMUEL 1:10–11

[Hannah] was in bitterness of soul, and prayed to the LORD and wept in anguish. Then she made a vow and said, "O LORD of hosts, if You will indeed look on the affliction of Your maidservant and remember me, and not forget Your maidservant, but will give Your maidservant a male child, then I will give him to the LORD all the days of his life, and no razor shall come upon his head."

Hannah's influence as an extraordinary woman of God is traceable to a second great love of her life (and definitely the most important): her love for God. Her desire for a child was no mere craving for self-gratification. It wasn't about her or getting what she wanted. It was about self-sacrifice—giving herself to that little life in order to give him back to the Lord. "No razor shall come upon his head" means that she would fulfill the first of three provisions of a Nazirite vow (Numbers 6:1–9). He would be a "set aside one" for life.

Hannah's spiritual passion can be seen in the fervency of her prayer life. She was a devout woman whose affections were set on heavenly things. She even begged God for a son who would be fit to serve in the tabernacle—not merely strong, healthy, handsome, or smart. She wanted a son with stellar character.

1 SAMUEL 1:13, 15

Now Hannah spoke in her heart; only her lips moved, but her voice was not heard. Therefore Eli thought she was drunk. . . . But Hannah answered and said, "No, my lord, I am a woman of sorrowful spirit. I have drunk neither wine nor intoxicating drink, but have poured out my soul before the LORD."

Because Hannah loved the Lord, she naturally turned to Him to plead her case. It was significant, I think, that despite the bitter agony Hannah suffered because of her childlessness, she never became a complainer or a nag. There's no suggestion that she ever grumbled against God or badgered her husband about her childlessness. Why should she complain to Elkanah? Children are an inheritance from the Lord. Therefore, Hannah took her case straight to the Lord. Despite her disappointment and heartache, she remained faithful to YHWH. In fact, frustration seems to have turned her more and more *to* the Lord, not *away* from Him. And she persisted in prayer.

The manner in which Hannah dealt with her sorrow and disappointment is a lesson for all of us. Rather than blame God for our troubles or turn away from Him in bitterness, trust that He cares and that He will do what is best.

1 SAMUEL 1:17–18

Then Eli answered and said, "Go in peace, and the God of Israel grant your petition which you have asked of Him." And she said, "Let your maidservant find favor in your sight." So the woman went her way and ate, and her face was no longer sad.

Hannah cast her whole burden upon the Lord and left her sense of frustration there at the altar. She did what she had come to the tabernacle to do. She had brought her case before the Lord. Now she was content to leave the matter in His hands.

Some people will pray, "O God, here's my problem," and then leave His presence in complete doubt and frustration, still shouldering the same burden they originally brought before the Lord, not really trusting Him to sustain them. Hannah truly laid her troubles in the lap of the Lord, totally confident that He would answer her in accord for what was best for her. There's a real humility in that kind of faith, as the apostle Peter noted: "Humble yourselves under the mighty hand of God, that He may exalt you in due time, casting all your care upon Him, for He cares for you" (1 Peter 5:6–7).

1 SAMUEL 2:1

And Hannah prayed and said:
"My heart rejoices in the LORD;
My horn is exalted in the LORD.
I smile at my enemies,
Because I rejoice in Your salvation."

When God finally did answer Hannah's prayer by giving her the son she had asked for, her thankful soul responded with a pure, unbroken stream of praise. Her words, recorded for us in 1 Samuel 2:1–10, reveal how thoroughly familiar Hannah was with the deep things of God. She acknowledged His holiness, His goodness, His sovereignty, His power, and His wisdom. She worshiped Him as Savior, as Creator, and as sovereign Judge. She acknowledged the fallenness and depravity of human nature, as well as the folly of unbelief and rebellion. In short, her few stanzas were a masterpiece of theological understanding.

While Hannah' knowledge was not mere academic theology, her words indicate that her knowledge of God was accurate— she saw Him as He is, not how she imagined, hoped, or wanted to see Him. Praying to a God we imagine and don't really know is not much better than idolatry. He's worth the effort to know accurately.

1 SAMUEL 1:22–23

Hannah did not go up [to the tabernacle], for she said to her husband, "Not until the child is weaned; then I will take him, that he may appear before the LORD and remain there forever." So Elkanah her husband said to her, "Do what seems best to you; wait until you have weaned him. Only let the LORD establish His word." Then the woman stayed and nursed her son until she had weaned him.

A third major characteristic of Hannah was her devotion to home and family. We see evidence of this in her love for Elkanah and his love for her. We see it in the way she rose above the petty strife and feuding of Peninnah. We see it again in Hannah's intense longing to be a mother. We see it best in how committed she was to her child in his early childhood. The time to surrender him to the Lord as she had promised would come soon enough—children were weaned around three years of age in that culture. Until then, she would savor every moment with her son.

Oh that more parents would be fully present during their children's early years. Hannah lived each day with her son knowing that their time was limited. This is true for all parents; unfortunately, they fail to appreciate the fact until it's too late.

Train up a child in the way he should go,
And when he is old he will not depart from it.

Hannah seemed to understand how vital those early years are, when 90 percent of personality is formed. She prepared Samuel in those formative years for a lifetime of service to God—the high calling to which she had consecrated him before he was ever born. History tells us that she did her job well. Samuel, obviously a precocious child, grew in wisdom and understanding. Those early years set a course for his life from which he never deviated.

Unfortunately, many parents wait until the teen years before fully engaging in their children's lives, and only then because their behavior has become too alarming to ignore. Of course, by then the best these parents can hope for is to help their teens survive long enough to correct the problems caused by a decade of neglect. Devoted parenting early on can't guarantee problems won't occur later, but tragedy is almost certain without it.

I SAMUEL 2:18–19

Samuel ministered before the LORD, even as a child, wearing a linen ephod.
Moreover his mother used to make him a little robe, and bring it to him year
by year when she came up with her husband to offer the yearly sacrifice.

While Hannah surrendered her son to the Lord, she didn't abandon him. Both parents remained meaningfully engaged in their son's life. In effect, the tabernacle became his boarding school and Eli his tutor. She and Elkanah naturally would have increased their visits to Shiloh and probably extended the duration of each visit too. Scripture states that she brought him a little robe "year by year," which doesn't mean "just once per year." It speaks of the regularity and faithfulness of their visits.

Hannah's experience is, of course, extraordinary. No one expects parents to hand over their children to the nearest church. However, her prayer is one that should be on the lips of every mother and father. And the principle of weaning a child to become a servant of God is one all parents would do well to apply. If you are a parent or you hope to be, let me challenge you to pray for your children's spiritual well-being now. It's never too early.

1 SAMUEL 2:20–21

[Each visit,] Eli would bless Elkanah and his wife, and say, "The LORD give you descendants from this woman for the loan that was given to the LORD." Then they would go to their own home. And the LORD visited Hannah, so that she conceived and bore three sons and two daughters. Meanwhile the child Samuel grew before the LORD.

When the Lord gives grace, He always outdoes Himself. Hannah prayed for a son. And then she honored her vow by surrendering her only child. Scripture says God blessed Hanah with five more children—three sons and two daughters. Her home and family life became rich and full. She was blessed by God to be allowed to achieve every ambition she had ever longed to fulfill. Her love for God, spouse, and home were still the true priorities of every godly wife and mother—every husband and father—that matter! Hannah's extraordinary life stands as a wonderful example to men and women who want their homes to be places where God is honored, even in the midst of a dark and sinful culture.

Hannah showed what the Lord can do through one woman totally and unreservedly devoted to Him.

May her tribe increase.

JOHN 1:45

Philip found Nathanael and said to him, "We have found Him of whom Moses in the law, and also the prophets, wrote—Jesus of Nazareth, the son of Joseph."

The combined gospel accounts tell us that Philip's closest companion was Nathanael ("God has given"), surname Bartholomew ("Son of Tolmai"). The information we have about Nathanael is limited; nevertheless, it reveals much about his character. Our first encounter tells us that the truth of Scripture was something that mattered to him. Philip knew his friend well, so he knew Nathanael would be intrigued by the news that Jesus was the One prophesied by Moses and the prophets. Naturally, this suggests that Nathanael *knew* the Old Testament prophecies. And, in all likelihood, the two men had come to the wilderness to hear John the Baptist in their search for the Messiah.

How strong is your commitment to truth? Are you willing to sacrifice your comfort for the sake of truth? How about your pride? Are you willing to be humbled by truth? What about wealth? If living in harmony with truth required losing most of what you own, would you accept the loss?

Does the truth of God rule your life? If not, what does?

Philip found Nathanael and said to him, "We have found Him of whom Moses in the law, and also the prophets, wrote—Jesus of Nazareth, the son of Joseph."

Note that Philip didn't say, "I found a man who has a wonderful plan for your life." He didn't say, "I found a man who will fix your marriage and your personal problems and give your life meaning." He didn't appeal to his companion on the basis of how Jesus might make *Nathanael's* life better. He approached the future disciple as an eager student of the Scriptures, a seeker of divine truth, a man who understood that the coming of Messiah was an event that would change the whole world.

While the Bible will indeed offer practical solutions to the problems of life, it is no mere self-help manual. The Scriptures are the means by which we come to know the Almighty! Let me challenge you to set aside your problems for a season and read God's Word with the sole purpose of knowing Him. I am confident that your life will never be the same.

COLOSSIANS 3:16

Let the word of Christ dwell in you richly in all wisdom, teaching and admonishing one another in psalms and hymns and spiritual songs, singing with grace in your hearts to the Lord.

It appears that all of the disciples, with the exception of Judas Iscariot, were to some degree already true seekers after divine truth before they met Jesus. Their hearts were open to the truth and hungry to know it. In that sense, they were different from the religious establishment, which was dominated by hypocrisy and false piety. These eleven men, including Nathanael, were the real thing.

Church membership—and even full-time Christian ministry—is not a reliable indicator of authentic piety. Churches and religious organizations are only as godly as the hearts of the people who lead and attend them. So the first and best way you can serve your local church body is to be a dogged seeker of truth, a person whose heart is open to teaching and sensitive to correction. And the most effective way to lead is to be the first to say, "I don't know," and then search the Scriptures to know the mind of God.

2 TIMOTHY 2:15

Be diligent to present yourself approved to God, a worker who does not need to be ashamed, rightly dividing the word of truth.

M ost likely, Philip and Nathanael had pored long hours over the Scriptures together, searching the Law and the Prophets to discern the truth about the coming of Messiah. And the fact that they were so well trained in Scripture no doubt explains why they were so quick to respond to Jesus. Nathanael, especially, was able to recognize Jesus clearly and instantly because he had a clear understanding of what the Bible had said about Him. He sized up Jesus quickly and received Him on the spot.

How quickly can you discern truth from fiction? Have you trained your mind to recognize the difference? Bible lessons on Sunday morning are a good start, and devotional materials can be very helpful during the week, but there's nothing like intensive, concentrated study in theology to tune your internal truth detector. Advanced training in Christian truth can be found in many churches, Bible colleges, and even online. Perhaps it's time to take your love of truth to the next level.

NO PLACE FOR PREJUDICE

And Nathanael said to him, "Can anything good come out of Nazareth?"
Philip said to him, "Come and see."

Although Nathanael had strong spiritual interests and had been faithful, diligent, and honest in his devotion to the Word of God, he was a fallen, imperfect man with certain prejudices. When Philip told him Jesus was the son of Joseph from the insignificant town of Nazareth, Nathanael *might* have said, "As I read the Old Testament, Micah the prophet says Messiah comes out of Bethlehem [Micah 5:2], not Nazareth." But the depth of his prejudice comes through in the words he chose. Note that Philip's response was not to argue, but to encourage a personal encounter with the Son of God.

Because we all are fallen, we all approach life with preconceptions and prejudgments that color our perception of the world. And more often than not, we are unaware of how our prejudices affect our ability to see truth. Education can certainly help, but not like having a personal relationship with the Author of truth. Our only real hope is for truth to take up residence in our hearts.

1 CORINTHIANS 1:27

But God has chosen the foolish things of the world to put to shame the wise, and God has chosen the weak things of the world to put to shame the things which are mighty.

Nathanael's objection was not a rational or biblical one; it was based on sheer emotion and bigotry, reflecting a kind of civic rivalry between Cana and Nazareth. It reveals what contempt the man had for the rough little town. Its culture was unrefined and uneducated, and it wasn't a particularly picturesque place. While Judeans looked down on all Galileans, Galileans looked down on Nazarenes.

Here again we see that God takes pleasure in using the common, weak, and lowly things of this world to confound the wise and powerful. In fact, He can even take a flawed person who is blinded by prejudice, and He can change that person into a means of divine good to transform the world.

I don't know about you, but that gives me great confidence that as long as I seek and serve the Lord with a whole heart, my flaws will never prevent the Lord from accomplishing great things through me. What a privilege to be His instrument!

But when the chief priests and scribes saw the wonderful things that [Jesus]
did, and the children crying out in the temple and saying, "Hosanna to the
Son of David!" they were indignant and said to Him, "Do You hear what
these are saying?" And Jesus said to them, "Yes. Have you never read, 'Out
of the mouth of babes and nursing infants You have perfected praise'?"

Prejudice is ugly. Generalizations based on feelings of superiority cut a lot of people off from the truth and can be spiritually debilitating. As a matter of fact, much of the nation of Israel rejected their Messiah because of prejudice. They did not believe their Messiah should come out of Nazareth, either. He had not been educated alongside the religious elite, and He preached a message that challenged and confounded their long-held beliefs.

Prejudice is really nothing more than prejudging the relative worth or competence of another based on a stereotype. And it need not be racial. Prejudice can be regional, geographical, educational, economic, or even denominational. Far better that we give each individual the benefit of doubt, weigh his or her beliefs against the teaching of Scripture, and respond in kindness with every encounter. Then, we might be surprised to discover profound truths from the most unexpected sources.

A soft answer turns away wrath,
But a harsh word stirs up anger.

Nathanael lived in a society that was prejudicial by temperament. In reality, all sinful people are. We make prejudicial statements. We draw prejudicial conclusions about individuals, about whole classes of people, and about truth itself. Nathanael, like the rest of us, had that sinful tendency. Fortunately, his prejudice wasn't strong enough to keep him from Christ. Instead of arguing or acting offended when Nathanael said, "Can anything good come out of Nazareth?" Philip said to him, "Come and see." That is a good way to deal with prejudice: Confront it with the facts. Prejudice is instinctual, conditioned, and feeling-based. So the remedy for prejudice is an honest look at objective reality through a personal encounter with truth.

As Christ's ambassadors, we should be more concerned about the truth itself than about how people feel about it—or even how they feel about *us*. "Come and see" is a great way to confront small-mindedness and closed-mindedness. But you must know the truth and be convinced of it yourself before you will be able to answer other people's prejudices persuasively.

JOHN 6:44

"No one can come to Me unless the Father who sent Me draws him; and I will raise him up at the last day."

Fortunately, Nathanael's prejudice wasn't strong enough to keep him from Christ. His closed mind wasn't as powerful as his seeking heart, and his hunger for truth overcame his bigotry. But I don't credit Nathanael for that. This was obviously the result of the Holy Spirit preparing the man to meet His Savior.

I have seen this very often in my experience with those in need of Christ. The Holy Spirit creates within them such desperate need that nothing—not family, not prejudice, not Satan, nor even their own skepticism—can keep them from the irresistible truth of Jesus Christ. Sometimes the more they resist, the more they protest, the harder they are inevitably drawn to what they cannot deny.

What a great means of evangelism! Pray for such divine misery and then gently invite, "Come and see."

JOHN 1:47

Jesus saw Nathanael coming toward Him, and said of him, "Behold, an Israelite indeed, in whom is no deceit!"

The most important aspect of Nathanael's character is expressed from the lips of Jesus. Jesus (who knew people's hearts) knew that Nathanael was already a justified man—a wholehearted believer in the truth, insofar as he understood it from the Old Testament. So Christ's first words upon seeing the man were a powerful commendation of his spiritual character: "Behold, an Israelite indeed, in whom is no deceit!"

Can you imagine a more wonderful thing than to have words of approval like that come out of the mouth of Jesus? It would be one thing to hear that at the end of your life, along with, "Well done, good and faithful servant." But how would you like Jesus to say that about you here and now?

In a true and vital sense, that is precisely Christ's present verdict with regard to every believer. That is what it means to be "justified": to be declared righteous by God, "the justifier of the one who has faith in Jesus" (Romans 3:26).

Blessed are the pure in heart,
For they shall see God.

Nathanael was pure-hearted in the sense that his faith was authentic. Certainly, he was fallen; he had sinful faults. His mind was tainted by a degree of prejudice. But his heart was not poisoned by the deceit of willful unbelief. He was a true believer; not a hypocrite. His love for God, and his desire to see the Messiah, were genuine. In that sense, his heart was sincere and without guile.

That's why Jesus referred to him as "an Israelite indeed." The Greek word is *alethos*, meaning "truly, genuinely." While Nathanael was an ethnic Israelite by virtue of his genetic link to Abraham, he was a true, genuine son of Abraham because he shared the faith of Abraham (Romans 4:16).

There are *lots* of people claiming to be Christian and, sadly, misrepresenting Christ to the world. But there are also multitudes who are "Christian indeed." We cannot always reliably tell them apart, but God knows whose faith is genuine, and He declares them fully righteous (Romans 4:4-8).

ROMANS 2:28–29

For he is not a Jew who is one outwardly, nor is circumcision that which is outward in the flesh; but he is a Jew who is one inwardly; and circumcision is that of the heart, in the Spirit, not in the letter; whose praise is not from men but from God.

The outward symbol of circumcision was a symbol of purification, and it was supposed to reflect a man's commitment to God, much like a wedding band symbolizes the exclusive devotion shared between a man and a woman. The rings are meaningless if the people are not genuinely devoted.

Nathanael was an authentic Jew, one of the true spiritual offspring of Abraham. Here was one who worshiped the true and living God without deceit and without hypocrisy, and that made Nathanael a rare man in first century Israel. The synagogues were full of hypocrites from the highest leaders to the people on the street. Hypocrisy was a plague in that culture. But here was a Jew whose heart was circumcised.

Hypocrisy in the church is no less a problem today and is perhaps a major contributor to unbelief. You don't need to be eloquent or outspoken. You don't need to be a Bible scholar or a brilliant theologian. If you really want to impact the world for Christ, be authentic in your faith and let your light shine (Matthew 5:14–16).

JOHN 1:48

Nathanael said to Him, "How do You know me?" Jesus answered and said to him, "Before Philip called you, when you were under the fig tree, I saw you."

At first, Nathanael was simply amazed that Jesus seemed to know anything about him, but this man from Nazareth didn't fit the picture of the Messiah Nathanael carried in his mind. Jesus was the son of a carpenter, a no-name, nondescript man from a town that had no connection to any prophecy. Yet He possessed uncanny knowledge of Nathanael's heart. That gave the disciple enough reason to set aside the messiah of his imagination to consider the stranger from Galilee. Because his heart was sincere and his faith was real, Nathanael overcame his prejudice.

Here is where the guilelessness of Nathanael's heart becomes obvious. He easily recognized the power and authority of Christ, because Christ knew his heart so well. Nathanael's instant submission to Christ is the model of what authentic faith should be.

How speedily do you surrender to Christ?

Nathanael said to Him, "How do You know me?" Jesus answered and said to him, "Before Philip called you, when you were under the fig tree, I saw you."

How do you know me?" He might have meant, "Are You just flattering me? Are You trying to make me one of Your followers by paying me compliments? How could You possibly know what is in my heart?" But Jesus' answer put a whole different spin on things. This was not flattery; it was omniscience! Jesus wasn't physically present to see Nathanael under the fig tree; Nathanael knew that. Suddenly he realized he was standing in the presence of Someone who could see into his very heart with an omniscient eye.

Mark Twain wrote, "Every one is a moon, and has a dark side which he never shows to anybody." But nothing is hidden from Christ. He sees all. Does this frighten you or comfort you? The answer to that question says a lot about your relationship with Him, whether it's agitated by shame or resting in trust.

PSALM 139:1–4

O LORD, You have searched me and known me.
You know my sitting down and my rising up;
You understand my thought afar off.
You comprehend my path and my lying down,
And are acquainted with all my ways.
For there is not a word on my tongue,
But behold, O LORD, You know it altogether.

What was the significance of the fig tree? It was most likely the place where Nathanael went to study and meditate on Scripture. If you wanted to escape the noise and stifling atmosphere of the house, you could go and rest under the shade of a fig tree. It was a kind of outdoor sanctuary, perfect for meditation, reflection, and solitude.

Because Jesus and His Father are one, He was saying, in effect, "I know the state of your heart because I saw you under the fig tree. I saw you in your secluded place, and I know what you keep in the private chambers of your heart." We have no way of knowing what Nathanael was thinking under that fig tree. Perhaps he was meditating on Psalm 139, where David celebrates God's ability to see into his heart. Whatever it was, Nathanael knew that Jesus knew, and that was enough to convince the guileless disciple. He said, "Rabbi, You are the Son of God!"

Nathanael answered and said to Him, "Rabbi, You are the Son of God! You are the King of Israel!"

Nathanael knew the Old Testament. He was familiar with what the prophets had said. He knew whom to look for. And now, regardless of the fact that Jesus came from Nazareth, His omniscience, His spiritual insight, His ability to read the heart of Nathanael was enough to convince Nathanael that He was indeed the true Messiah. As a careful student of Scripture, he knew that when Messiah came He would be Son of God and King.

Nathanael was never one of the half committed. He came to full understanding and total commitment on one day. His heart was prepared so that complete trust quickly followed recognition. And that is how it should be.

In what do you trust? Your Savior or your income? To what are you committed? Your King or your own way? In whom do you hope? In God, or in someone else? The right answers to those questions define authentic faith.

PROVERBS 9:10

The fear of the LORD is the beginning of wisdom,
And the knowledge of the Holy One is understanding.

Jesus affirmed Nathanael's faith and promised that he would see even greater things than a simple show of Jesus' omniscience. If one simple statement about the fig tree was enough to convince Nathanael that this was the Son of God and the King of Israel, he had not seen anything yet. From here on out, everything he would see would enrich and enlarge his faith.

Faith is not a destination; it is a birth into the kind of life God intended. It is the beginning of growth, like the germination of a seed. Moreover, faith is a manner of life that results in a growing confidence in the love and care of your Creator.

Your confidence may be unsure, your assurance feeble. Let me encourage you to devote yourself to knowing God more intimately through Scripture study, meditation, prayer, worship, and fellowship with other believers. In time, your confidence in Him will grow. Believe me, you haven't seen anything yet!

JOHN 1:50

Jesus answered and said to him, "Because I said to you, 'I saw you under the fig tree,' do you believe? You will see greater things than these."

Most of the disciples struggled just to come to the place where Nathanael stood after his first meeting with Christ. But for Nathanael, the ministry of Jesus only affirmed what he already knew to be true. How wonderful to see someone so trustworthy and trusting from the very beginning, so that for him the whole three years with Jesus was just an unfolding panorama of supernatural reality!

Augustine wrote, "We believed in order to know; for if we wanted to know first, and then to believe, we should not be able either to know or to believe." The life of faith is not a gathering of knowledge in order to believe. It begins with the decision to trust in Christ and then grows richer and deeper as we experience Him through life. Trust, therefore, is a moral decision more than an intellectual one.

And [Jesus] said to [Nathanael], "Most assuredly, I say to you, hereafter you shall see heaven open, and the angels of God ascending and descending upon the Son of Man."

M ost Jews at this time were hoping for a Messiah who would destroy their enemies, free their land from dominion, bring prosperity again to Israel, and then rule over the whole world. Christ will indeed do all of that in the future. But first, He came to establish "peace with God" (Romans 5:1). Unlike his contemporaries, Nathanael longed for peace with God more than anything else. Jesus knew this and assured Nathanael he had found what he was looking for.

In the Old Testament, Jacob had a dream in which "a ladder was set up on the earth, and its top reached to heaven; and there the angels of God were ascending and descending on it" (Genesis 28:12). Jesus' words to Nathanael were a reference to that ancient account. *He* is the ladder that connects heaven and earth.

LUKE 16:10

He who is faithful in what is least is faithful also in much; and he who is unjust in what is least is unjust also in much.

We don't know much about Nathanael beyond what John reveals in his gospel. Early church records suggest that he ministered in Persia and India and took the gospel as far as Armenia. There is no reliable record of how he died. One tradition says he was tied up in a sack and cast into the sea. Another tradition says he was crucified. By all accounts, he was martyred like all the apostles except John.

What we do know is that Nathanael was faithful to the end because he was faithful from the start. Everything he experienced with Christ and whatever he experienced after the birth of the New Testament church ultimately only made his faith stronger. And Nathanael, like the other apostles, stands as proof that God can take the most common people, from the most insignificant places, and use them for His glory.

1 CORINTHIANS 1:26–27

For you see your calling, brethren, that not many wise according to the
flesh, not many mighty, not many noble, are called. But God has chosen the
foolish things of the world to put to shame the wise, and God has chosen the
weak things of the world to put to shame the things which are mighty.

One of the facts that stands out in the lives of all twelve apostles is how ordinary and unrefined they were when Jesus met them. All twelve, with the exception of Judas Iscariot, were from Galilee. That whole region was predominantly rural, consisting of small towns and villages. Its people were not elite. They were not known for their education. They were the commonest of the common. They were fishermen and farmers. Such were the disciples as well. Christ deliberately passed over those who were aristocratic and influential and chose men mostly from the dregs of society.

If Jesus could take such rabble from the backwoods of Galilee and transform them into a world-changing spiritual force, what might He do with us if only we would be willing to follow without reservation?

AMOS 5:21–24

"I hate, I despise your feast days, and I do not savor your sacred assemblies. Though you offer Me burnt offerings and your grain offerings, I will not accept them, nor will I regard your fattened peace offerings. Take away from Me the noise of your songs, for I will not hear the melody of your stringed instruments. But let justice run down like water, and righteousness like a mighty stream."

It should be no surprise that Christ disdained religious elitism. The religious leaders of Jesus' day (like the vast majority of religious celebrities even today) were blind leaders of the blind. Most members of the Jewish establishment in Jesus' day were so spiritually blind that when the Messiah came and did miracles before their eyes, they still did not see Him as the Messiah. They saw Him rather as an interloper and an intruder. They regarded Him as an enemy. And from the very outset, from the first time He preached in public, they sought a way to have Him murdered.

It's a sure sign of hypocrisy when religiosity displaces genuine worship, when rituals replace relationship. God is not impressed by pomp or ceremony. Pageants will never distract Him from His true desire. He wants hearts that are committed to Him. He wants people who seek Him and who know Him and who respond with authentic devotion. Then—and only then—will our services offer true worth-ship to the Lord.

PSALM 138:6

Though the LORD is on high,
Yet He regards the lowly;
But the proud He knows from afar.

In the end, it was the chief priests and ruling council of Israel who led the crowd in a cry for Jesus' blood. The religious establishment hated Him. So it is no wonder that when the time came for Jesus to choose and appoint apostles, He looked away from the religious elite and chose instead simple men of faith who were, by earthly standards, commonplace. Whereas the religious elite could not tolerate being called sinners, the ordinary men Jesus chose to be His apostles were not reluctant to acknowledge their own sinfulness.

Those are the kind of people churches need to have in leadership; men and women who are willing to stand before others, admit their own continuing need for the Savior, and faithfully point others to Christ.

ISAIAH 53:2−3

For He shall grow up before Him as a tender plant, and as a root out of dry ground. He has no form or comeliness; and when we see Him, there is no beauty that we should desire Him. He is despised and rejected by men, a Man of sorrows and acquainted with grief. And we hid, as it were, our faces from Him; He was despised, and we did not esteem Him.

It is truly remarkable that when Jesus was born, so few people in Israel recognized their Messiah. It was not as if no one was watching for Him. Messianic expectation in the early first century was running at an all-time high. Virtually all faithful believers in Israel were already expectantly awaiting the Messiah. The irony is that so very few recognized Him because He met none of their expectations. They were looking for a mighty political and military leader.

The only people in Israel who did recognize Christ at His birth were humble, unremarkable people. The Magi, the shepherds, an old man in the temple named Simeon, and an equally aged woman named Anna. The politically powerful and religious elite—those who preferred to keep things as they were—didn't know the long-awaited Messiah had arrived, because they weren't looking.

MALACHI 3:1

"Behold, I send My messenger,
And he will prepare the way before Me.
And the Lord, whom you seek,
Will suddenly come to His temple,
Even the Messenger of the covenant,
In whom you delight. Behold, He is coming,"
Says the LORD *of hosts.*

M ary and Joseph entered the temple cradling their child, undoubtedly along with dozens of other parents. Their purpose was to dedicate Jesus as the Law had prescribed. Simeon had just picked up the infant Jesus and pronounced a prophetic blessing on Him. In that instant, Anna happened by and immediately understood what was going on and who Christ was. Perhaps she overheard Simeon's blessing. She stopped and took notice when she heard the joyous blessing he pronounced on Jesus.

Anna was far from being the most educated, influential, or well-known woman in Israel. But she knew the scriptures and her heart was expectant. God graciously gave her the privilege of recognizing Christ as the long-awaited Savior many years before He revealed Himself to anyone else.

LUKE 2:37

This woman was a widow of about eighty-four years, who did not depart from the temple, but served God with fastings and prayers night and day.

By the time of Jesus' birth, Anna was already advanced in years. She had not enjoyed a particularly easy life. Her whole world was shattered by tragedy when she was still quite young, apparently before she had even borne children. Her husband died seven years after their marriage, and she had remained single ever since. At eighty-four years of age, she had been a widow for more than six decades in a society in which widowhood virtually guaranteed a life of extreme poverty.

No one can say for certain, but it is likely Anna *chose* to remain unmarried. If she was married at the customary age of thirteen, she would have been twenty when her husband died and very eligible for remarriage. Instead, it appears she turned her tragedy into an opportunity to serve the Lord full-time in the temple, teaching and encouraging other women and interceding on behalf of her people.

"Know therefore and understand,
That from the going forth of the command
To restore and build Jerusalem
Until Messiah the Prince,
There shall be seven weeks [49 years] and sixty-two weeks [434 years]."

Luke said that Anna never left the temple, which was probably a literal statement. She could have lived right there on the temple grounds in one of the apartments on the outer court typically utilized by out-of-town priests when they served their two weeks' annual service. Perhaps because of her long faithfulness, her obvious spiritual gifts, her steadfast devotion to the Lord, and her constant commitment to her ministry of prayer and fasting, temple officials had given her a chamber.

Anna knew the Messiah was coming, and that it would be in her lifetime. The prophet Daniel predicted the year of the Christ's suffering, from which faithful Jews could surmise the approximate time of His birth. The imminent arrival of the Messiah in the temple would have made leaving the premises unappealing, even for a short time. Undoubtedly, this was the primary reason she fasted and prayed. While the scholars quibbled over man-made customs, Anna studied the Scriptures and watched the temple gate.

LUKE 2:36–37

Now there was one, Anna, a prophetess, the daughter of Phanuel, of the tribe of Asher. She was of a great age, and had lived with a husband seven years from her virginity; and this woman was a widow of about eighty-four years.

Luke introduced Anna as "a prophetess," meaning that she faithfully spoke the Word of God. This is not to say she predicted the future or even that she received special revelation from God. In fact, any preacher who faithfully proclaims the written Word of God would be a "prophet" in the general biblical sense. Anna may have been a teacher of the Old Testament to other women. And this gift for proclaiming God's truth ultimately played a major role in the ministry she is still best remembered for.

Anna had already consistently and accurately taught God's truth for longer than most people live. Her thorough knowledge of the Scriptures and her faithfulness in teaching others had also prepared her to receive the Christ with a whole heart. This experience must have set her heart aflame with zeal for the Redeemer, and surely for the rest of her life, He remained at the center of everything she taught.

And coming in that instant she gave thanks to the Lord, and spoke of Him to all those who looked for redemption in Jerusalem.

After decades of fasting and praying for the coming of Messiah, the answer to Anna's prayers had come in flesh and blood. Suddenly, her prophetic giftedness came boldly to the forefront. The verb tense signifies continuous action, meaning that she continually spoke of Him to all who were looking for the Redeemer. This became her one message for the rest of her life.

Notice that Anna knew who the believing remnant were. She could identify the *true* worshipers—the ones who, like her, were expectantly awaiting the Messiah. She sought people out, and every opportunity from then on, she spoke to them about *Him*. The Messiah had finally come, and Anna was one of the very first to know who He was. She thus became one of the very first and most enduring witnesses of Christ.

ECCLESIASTES 9:17

Words of the wise, spoken quietly, should be heard
Rather than the shout of a ruler of fools.

M atthew was also called by his Jewish name, "Levi the son of Alphaeus." He is, of course, the author of the gospel that bears his name. For that reason, we might expect to have a lot of detail about this man and his character. But we know very little because he was a humble, self-effacing man who kept himself almost completely in the background throughout his lengthy account of Jesus' life and ministry. In his entire gospel he mentions his own name only two times: once where he records his call and the other when he lists all twelve disciples.

People of quiet, self-effacing dignity are a treasure all too frequently ignored when we need their riches most. Their wisdom is seldom heard amid the prattling of attention-seekers who tend to dominate group settings. Learn to spot these soft-spoken sages and then coax out their perspectives by asking questions, both publicly and privately. Everyone will thank you later.

LUKE 5:27–28

After these things [Jesus] went out and saw a tax collector named Levi, sitting at the tax office. And He said to him, "Follow Me." So he left all, rose up, and followed Him.

Matthew was a tax collector—a publican—when Jesus called him. Tax collectors were the most despised people in Israel. They were hated and vilified by all of Jewish society. They were deemed lower than Herodians (Jews loyal to the Idumean dynasty of Herods) and more worthy of scorn than the occupying Roman soldiers. Publicans were men who had bought tax franchises from the Roman emperor and then extorted money from their own countrymen to feed Roman coffers and to pad their own pockets. They often strong-armed money out of people with the use of thugs. Most were despicable, vile, unprincipled scoundrels. "Tax collector" is the last credential we might expect to see from a man who would become an apostle of Christ, a top leader in the church, and a preacher of the gospel.

Obviously, Jesus judged qualifications according to a very different standard. He saw into the heart of each disciple, and He saw each man's future perfectly. The same is true for all of His chosen. What do you think He sees in your future?

LUKE 5:29

Then Levi gave Him a great feast in his own house. And there were a great number of tax collectors and others who sat down with them.

After Matthew decided to leave everything behind to follow Jesus, he hosted an enormous banquet to honor his new Master. He invited a large number of his fellow tax collectors and various other kinds of scoundrels and social outcasts to meet Jesus. As we saw in the case of Philip and Andrew, Matthew's first impulse after following Jesus was to bring his closest friends and introduce them to the Savior. He was so thrilled to have found the Messiah that he wanted to introduce Jesus to everyone he knew.

That's a natural reaction when you've discovered something wonderful. You can't wait to share it with anyone whose life might be improved. We tell others where they can find a great bargain. We want everyone to know about the latest miracle cure. But in this case, we've found *someone* wonderful. Why wouldn't we want everyone to know Him? Whom have you told lately?

LUKE 11:33

"No one, when he has lit a lamp, puts it in a secret place or under a basket, but on a lampstand, that those who come in may see the light."

Why did Matthew invite tax collectors and other lowlifes? Because they were the only kind of people he knew. They were the only ones who would associate with a man like Matthew. He didn't know any of the social elite well enough to invite them to his house. He was a tax collector, which put him on the same social level as harlots. For a Jewish man like Matthew, to be a tax collector was even worse. His occupation made him a traitor to the nation, a social pariah, the rankest of the rank. He would also have been a religious outcast, forbidden to enter any synagogue.

When Matthew first began to share the good news, he naturally began with the people he knew: fellow outcasts. People beyond the reach—or the concern—of the temple. The hopelessly lost. The very people Jesus came to save.

Perhaps your circle of acquaintances, friends, and family would be a good place to start sharing the good news. Not qualified? Neither was Matthew. Untrained? Inexperienced? So was Matthew.

PROVERBS 16:18

Pride goes before destruction,
And a haughty spirit before a fall.

Luke records what happened during Matthew's celebration. A collection of scribes and Pharisees gathered outside his home and lodged a complaint with Jesus' disciples. "Why do you eat and drink with the tax collectors and sinners?" Jesus answered and said to them, "Those who are well have no need of a physician, but those who are sick. I have not come to call the righteous, but sinners, to repentance" (Luke 5:31–32).

The greatest obstacle to belief in Jesus Christ is not ignorance; it's pride. It is not an intellectual dilemma; it's a moral defect. Trust in Christ requires one to admit his or her inability to become good enough for heaven. Therefore, those who think they have no need of Christ will refuse to accept His free gift of eternal life and scorn those who do.

MATTHEW 21:31–32

Jesus said to them, "Assuredly, I say to you that tax collectors and harlots enter the kingdom of God before you. For John came to you in the way of righteousness, and you did not believe him; but tax collectors and harlots believed him; and when you saw it, you did not afterward relent and believe him."

It is interesting to note that three tax collectors are specifically mentioned in the Gospels, and each one of them found forgiveness. There was Zacchaeus, in Luke 19:2–10; the publican mentioned in the parable of Luke 18:10–14; and Matthew. Conversely, the religious elite rarely even sought forgiveness. Jesus admonished them, saying the dregs of society will see heaven before the most doggedly religious people in the world.

How ironic, how tragically sad that a deluded devotion to self-righteous religion should keep so many from their God.

LUKE 18:14

"I tell you, this [tax collector] went to his house justified rather than the [Pharisee]; for everyone who exalts himself will be humbled, but he who humbles himself will be exalted."

In Jesus' parable in which a tax collector and a Pharisee worship at the temple, the tax collector stood "afar off." He had to. He would not have been permitted past the court of the Gentiles in the temple. In fact, tax collectors had to keep their distance from any group because they were so hated. The Jewish Talmud taught that it was righteous to lie and deceive a tax collector because that was what a professional extortioner deserved.

Matthew was in essence worse off religiously than a Gentile, so it must have been a stunning reality when Jesus chose him to become His disciple. Therefore, Matthew would have understood better than most the irony of Jesus' parable. Whereas religious pride brought one man to the temple only to praise himself, genuine humility kept another at a distance only to be found by God.

LUKE 5:27–28

After these things He went out and saw a tax collector named Levi, sitting at the tax office. And He said to him, "Follow Me." So he left all, rose up, and followed Him.

What was it in a man like Matthew that caused him to drop everything at once like that? We might assume he was a materialist. And at one time he must have been, or he never would have gotten into a position like that in the first place. So why would he walk away from everything and follow Jesus, not knowing what the future held?

The best answer we can deduce is that down deep inside he was a Jew who knew and loved the Old Testament. At some point in his life, most likely *after* he had chosen his despicable career, he was smitten with a gnawing spiritual hunger and became a true seeker. Of course, God was seeking and drawing *him*, and the gentle force of that pull was irresistible.

As you think about the people you know who do not know the Savior, how might the Lord be drawing them to Himself? How might you gently guide them in the right direction?

HEBREWS 4:12–13

The word of God is living and powerful, and sharper than any two-edged
sword, piercing even to the division of soul and spirit, and of joints and
marrow, and is a discerner of the thoughts and intents of the heart. And there
is no creature hidden from His sight, but all things are naked and open to the
eyes of Him to whom we must give account.

Matthew obviously knew the Old Testament very well; his gospel quotes the Old Testament ninety-nine times, which is more often than Mark, Luke, and John combined. He quotes out of the Law, out of the Psalms, and out of the Prophets—every section of the Old Testament. He must have studied the Scriptures on his own, because he couldn't hear the Word of God explained in any synagogue. Apparently, in a quest to fill the spiritual void in his life, he had turned to the Scriptures.

The Lord had thus prepared Matthew's heart for the day he first heard God in human flesh speak new truth. How the words of Jesus must have resonated with the Scripture Matthew had hidden in his heart!

Never underestimate the power of God's Word, especially when meditated upon and then added to one's memory banks. Think of how you might tactfully share the gift of God's Word with people you know to be lost.

PSALM 30:11–12

You have turned for me my mourning into dancing;
You have put off my sackcloth and clothed me with gladness,
To the end that my glory may sing praise to You and not be silent. O LORD
my God, I will give thanks to You forever.

Matthew's path through life was crooked, and it took him through some difficult and dark terrain, yet it led him straight to his Savior and it prepared him for an utterly unique ministry. He stands as a vivid reminder that the Lord often chooses the most despicable people of this world, redeems them, gives them new hearts, and uses them in remarkable ways to redeem yet more needy individuals.

You may prefer to forget your life before Christ, perhaps because the shame and regret are too unpleasant. But have you considered how the Lord might use those circumstances to bring others to Himself? Rather than cursing the path that led you to Christ, why not let Him turn it into a means of redemption in the life of another? Your regrets might lead another to the gift of eternal life. Let me challenge you to lay this matter before God in prayer, asking Him to use your sorrow to bring rejoicing to another. The gift you give might very well become healing for yourself.

LAMENTATIONS 3:22-23

Through the LORD's mercies we are not consumed,
Because His compassions fail not.
They are new every morning;
Great is Your faithfulness.

While the information we have on Matthew is scant in the New Testament, we nevertheless know a lot about his character. He knew the Old Testament, he believed in God, he looked for the Messiah, he dropped everything immediately when he met Jesus, and in the joy of his newfound relationship, he embraced the outcasts of his world and introduced them to Jesus. He became a man of quiet humility who loved the outcasts and gave no place to religious hypocrisy. His path to Christ had shaped his ministry as a disciple.

Because we each come to Christ with different experiences—some tragic, some fortunate—we each contribute uniquely to the new kingdom and the cause of the gospel. The challenge is to admire other believers and learn from them without feeling the need to imitate anyone other than Christ. While the sinful and shameful aspects of your past have been removed, how do you see your own path to the Savior influencing your ministry to others today?

[Jesus] said to them, "Those who are well have no need of a physician, but those who are sick. But go and learn what this means: 'I desire mercy and not sacrifice.' For I did not come to call the righteous, but sinners, to repentance."

Forgiveness is the thread that runs through Matthew 9 after the account of Matthew's conversion. Of course, even as a tax collector, he knew his sin, his greed, his betrayal of his own people. He knew he was guilty of graft, extortion, oppression, and abuse. But when Jesus said to him, "Follow Me," Matthew knew there was inherent in that command a promise of the forgiveness of his sin. His heart had long hungered for such forgiveness, which could not be found among the supposedly devoted worshipers of God in the temple. That is why he arose without hesitation and devoted the rest of his life to following Christ.

When people place your name alongside the name of Christ, do they see forgiveness in action? Do you openly live in gratitude for the forgiveness made possible by the sacrifice of God's Son? Do you extend that same forgiveness to others?

MATTHEW 10:24−25

[Jesus said], "A disciple is not above his teacher, nor a servant above his master. It is enough for a disciple that he be like his teacher, and a servant like his master. If they have called the master of the house Beelzebub, how much more will they call those of his household!"

We know that Matthew wrote his gospel with a Jewish audience in mind. Tradition says he ministered to the Jews both in Israel and abroad for many years before being martyred for his faith. There is no reliable record of how he was put to death, but the earliest traditions indicate he was burned at the stake. Thus this man who walked away from a lucrative career without ever giving it a second thought remained willing to give his all for Christ to the very end.

Jesus warned His followers that discipleship would be costly, at least in terms of how the world counts cost. Matthew didn't place much value on material things once he left his publican's office. What he gained in return are eternal riches that can never be lost.

So may it be with you. May you gladly relinquish what is fleeting and vain for that which is eternal and substantial: unrestricted access to all that is God's.

JOHN 4:3-4

[Jesus] left Judea and departed again to Galilee. But He needed to go through Samaria.

Samaritans were a mixed-race people descended from pagans who had intermarried with the few remaining Israelites after the Assyrians conquered the Northern Kingdom in 722 BC. By the first century, the Samaritans had a distinct culture built around syncretistic religion, blending aspects of Judaism and rank paganism. So the Jews' contempt for Samaritans was so intense that most simply refused to travel through Samaria, choosing to take a significantly longer route around their territory. But Jesus deliberately broke with convention. He had a purpose to fulfill, a troubled, outcast woman to redeem. Therefore, John's gospel tells us He "*needed* to go through Samaria."

This phrase—perhaps as much as any in the Gospels—illustrates Jesus' mission to planet Earth. A desperately down-and-out person needed redemption and her heart was ready to hear the good news of the Messiah. Jesus intentionally went out of His way to find and rescue the lost soul.

JOHN 4:7, 9

A woman of Samaria came to draw water. Jesus said to her, "Give Me a drink." . . . Then the woman of Samaria said to Him, "How is it that You, being a Jew, ask a drink from me, a Samaritan woman?" For Jews have no dealings with Samaritans."

Jesus met the Samaritan woman at a historic well, and His conversation with her started out simply and naturally enough—He asked for a drink. While she wasn't offended, she was nonetheless surprised. Gender taboos, racial divisions, and the class system would normally keep a man of Jesus' status from conversing with a woman such as she, much less drinking from a water container that belonged to her.

A common misunderstanding among nonbelievers is that one must first make himself or herself more acceptable before coming to Christ. This is not only unnecessary, it's impossible. The woman could do nothing to change her race, gender or social caste. Similarly, we are powerless to become anything other than sinful, depraved, morally helpless people.

In the same way, the Lord approached the Samaritan woman where she was, as she was, He comes to us where we are, as we are.

JOHN 4:10, 14

Jesus answered and said to her, "If you knew the gift of God, and who it is
who says to you, 'Give Me a drink,' you would have asked Him, and He
would have given you living water. . . . but whoever drinks of the water that
I shall give him will never thirst. But the water that I shall give him will
become in him a fountain of water springing up into everlasting life."

Jesus was indeed thirsty, but his true intention was to accomplish
His mission: to quench the thirst of the Samaritan woman's
soul. He spoke of Himself in metaphorical terms as the answer to
her soul's deepest need. She understood that He was speaking of
spiritual water and expressed her desire to be refreshed. However,
her coy reply suggests that she wasn't taking the Lord's offer seriously, probably because she didn't associate her "thirst" with her
guilt. She was a sinner who needed forgiveness.

The most difficult task in evangelism is getting people to recognize their sin, and therefore their need for the Savior. Churches
are filled with people who think that regular attendance, generous
giving, and diligent service make them good enough for heaven.
Week after week they hear the offer of salvation by grace through
faith, fail to acknowledge their need, and return home as lost and
as thirsty as when they came.

JOHN 4:17–18

The woman answered and said, "I have no husband." Jesus said to her, "You have well said, 'I have no husband,' for you have had five husbands, and the one whom you now have is not your husband; in that you spoke truly."

Jesus' next words unexpectedly drew her up short: "Go, call your husband, and come here." She immediately grew solemn. Jesus had exposed her need. The truth about her life was so horrible that she could not admit it to Him. Instead of exposing her disgrace to this rabbi, she told him only a small fraction of the truth. But to her utter chagrin, He knew the full truth already.

I love the low-key, almost droll simplicity with which she acknowledged her own guilt: "Sir, I perceive that You are a prophet." He had unmasked her completely. And yet, far from spurning her or castigating her, He had offered her the Water of Life!

Hiding our sin from God is pointless. He sees every infinitesimal detail of our depravity, and He boldly confronts us, not to be cruel, but to offer forgiveness and healing. Why would we want to hide from such love?

JOHN 4:25–26

The woman said to Him, "I know that Messiah is coming" (who is called Christ). "When He comes, He will tell us all things." Jesus said to her, "I who speak to you am He."

I s it not significant that this Samaritan woman, born and raised in a culture of corrupt religion, had the same messianic hope shared by every other godly woman in Scripture? She knew the Messiah was coming. It was embryonic faith waiting to be born. Then Jesus demonstrated His full knowledge of all her secrets, which confirmed His identity beyond any shadow of doubt.

The Holy Spirit was working in her heart. God the Father was drawing her irresistibly to Christ, revealing truth to her that eye had never seen and ear had never heard. In response to her sincere desire to know the Messiah, Jesus made the single most direct and explicit messianic claim He ever made—not to a disciple, not to the high priest, not to the august body of theological minds in Jerusalem, but to an "unworthy" woman of the lowest social rank in the worst moral condition.

JOHN 4:28–30

The woman then left her waterpot, went her way into the city, and said to the men, "Come, see a Man who told me all things that I ever did. Could this be the Christ?" Then they went out of the city and came to Him.

Soon after Jesus' revelation of His true identity, the woman left the well, leaving behind her waterpot. It wasn't absentmindedness that caused her to leave it; she fully intended to return. Her plan was to bring the leading men of the city and introduce them to Christ. She was privy to amazing knowledge that must not be kept secret.

Her response was typical of new believers, one of the evidences of authentic faith. The person who has just had the burden of sin and guilt lifted always wants to share the good news with others. She told the men of the city everything. No longer was she evading the facts of her sin. She was basking in the glow of forgiveness, and there is simply no shame in that.

JOHN 4:39–40

And many of the Samaritans of that city believed in Him because of the word of the woman who testified, "He told me all that I ever did." So when the Samaritans had come to Him, they urged Him to stay with them; and He stayed there two days.

The immediate impact of the Samaritan woman's testimony on her city, Sychar, was profound. They believed! What a contrast this makes with the reception Jesus received from the scribes and Pharisees in Jerusalem. They complained that Jesus received sinners and socialized with them. They were disgusted with Him because He was willing to converse with rogues and scoundrels such as this woman.

Because Samaritans lacked the phony scruples of religious hypocrisy, the Samaritan city experienced genuine revival, and it must have utterly transformed that little town. Jesus had indeed found a true worshiper—after her heart was changed by her encounter with Him. And then He found a whole town of true worshipers as a result of her extraordinary witness.

MATTHEW 19:30

"But many who are first will be last, and the last first."

The ninth name in Luke's list of the apostles is "James the son of Alphaeus" (Luke 6:15). The only thing Scripture tells us about this man is his name. If he ever wrote anything, it is lost to history. If he ever asked Jesus any questions or did anything to stand out from the group, Scripture does not record it. He never attained any degree of fame or notoriety. He was not the kind of person who stands out. He was utterly obscure. In fact, his lack of prominence appears to be reflected in his nickname, "James the Less." The Greek word is *mikros*, meaning "small."

Perhaps you are one who works in the background, faithfully contributing with little notice and even less thanks. Because our culture celebrates some roles while overlooking others, you might even feel insignificant. Fortunately, there are no insignificant people in Christ's kingdom. On the contrary, the "little" people in this age will receive the greatest honor of all.

MARK 10:29–30

So Jesus answered and said, "Assuredly, I say to you, there is no one who has left house or brothers or sisters or father or mother or wife or children or lands, for My sake and the gospel's, who shall not receive a hundredfold now in this time—houses and brothers and sisters and mothers and children and lands, with persecutions—and in the age to come, eternal life."

M*ikros* has the primary meaning, "small in stature," referring to his physical features. Perhaps "James the Less" was a short or small-framed man. The word can also speak of someone who is young in age. But the name most likely refers to his influence. As we have already seen, James the son of Zebedee was a man of prominence, while "Little James" stayed mostly in the background.

When you choose to serve, do you prefer up-front roles or behind-the-scenes work? Both are necessary. Neither is inherently more spiritual than the other. Self-doubt isn't more righteous than attention seeking; both can be forms of pride in which *self* is the central motivating factor.

The key is to make the best use of whatever gifts God has given you in a way that will best meet needs in your circle of influence—and be sure that all the glory goes to the Giver of those gifts.

ACTS 1:8

[Jesus said,] "You shall receive power when the Holy Spirit has come upon you; and you shall be witnesses to Me in Jerusalem, and in all Judea and Samaria, and to the end of the earth."

The disciples' importance did not stem from their pedigree. Had that been important, Scripture would have recorded it for us. What made these men important was the Lord whom they served and the message they proclaimed. If we lack details about the men themselves, that is Okay. Heaven will reveal the full truth of who they were and what they were like. In the meantime, it is enough to know that they were chosen by the Lord, empowered by the Spirit, and called by God to carry the gospel to the world of their day.

Interesting, isn't it? What made these men special is also true of you—if you are a believer. Do you serve the Lord and faithfully bear His message? Are you chosen by God, empowered by His Spirit, and called to carry the gospel to the world in your day? (If you are a believer, the answer is "Yes!")

Take a few moments now to reflect on what this says about your importance and your responsibility in building the kingdom.

JOHN 3:30-31

[John, the Baptist said,] "He must increase, but I must decrease. He who comes from above is above all; he who is of the earth is earthly and speaks of the earth. He who comes from heaven is above all.

All the disciples more or less disappear from the biblical narrative within a few years after Pentecost. In no case does Scripture give us a full biography. That is because Scripture always keeps the focus on the power of Christ and the power of the Word, not the men who were merely instruments of that power. These men were filled with the Spirit, and they preached the Word. That is all we really need to know. The vessel is not the issue; the Master is.

True greatness can be found only in submission to God. The Son became the ultimate example of this when He laid aside all the privileges of deity to become a man and to serve the Father as humankind was created to do. Those of His followers who understood His message and followed His example became great in their smallness before God. Their example is now your invitation.

LUKE 10:38

Now it happened as they went that He entered a certain village; and a certain woman named Martha welcomed Him into her house.

Martha and Mary make a fascinating pair—very different in many ways but alike in one vital respect: both of them loved Christ. They became cherished personal friends of Jesus during His earthly ministry. Moreover, He had a profound love for their family, which included their brother Lazarus.

We're not told how this particular household became so intimate with Jesus. It seems likely that Martha and Mary were simply two of the many people who heard Jesus teach early in His ministry, extended Him hospitality, and built a relationship with Him in that way. Regardless, it is clear from Luke's description that Jesus made Himself at home in their home.

He was their Lord, and thus an honored guest in their midst. He was also their cherished friend, so close and beloved as to be virtually a member of their household. That is a fitting metaphor for His relationship with every believer (John 15:14).

JOHN 12:3

Then Mary took a pound of very costly oil of spikenard, anointed the feet of Jesus, and wiped His feet with her hair. And the house was filled with the fragrance of the oil.

Mary, Martha's sister, is best remembered for anointing the feet of Jesus during a sizable dinner party, at which Martha appears to be the acting hostess. It took place in the home of a well-to-do, former leper by the name of Simon, who may have been a close friend of the family. During dinner, Mary poured out nearly a year's wages worth of ointment on Jesus' feet and then wiped His feet with her hair as she worshiped and wept. Jesus' willingness to accept such a lavish expression of worship is what finally sealed Judas's decision to betray Christ.

The same is true today. The sincere, unguarded worship of some will incite others to anger. In fact, some atheists have labeled all belief in God a menace to human progress and have determined to rid the world of worship altogether. Nevertheless, the sweet fragrance of worship continues to rise.

LUKE 10:41–42

Jesus answered and said to her, "Martha, Martha, you are worried and troubled about many things. But one thing is needed, and Mary has chosen that good part, which will not be taken away from her."

There could be no more gracious host than Martha, who fussed over the details of hospitality, making certain everything was right. Much in her behavior was commendable. And Jesus was the perfect houseguest, instantly making Himself at home. No doubt His disciples were asking Him questions, and He was giving answers that were authoritative and edifying. Mary's instinct was to sit at His feet and listen. Martha, ever the fastidious one, went right to work with her preparations.

Soon, however, Martha grew irritable with Mary for failing to help, and finally complained to Jesus, asking Him to intervene and set Mary straight. Jesus' reply must have startled Martha. And, no doubt, the gentle rebuke penetrated her heart and had exactly the sanctifying effect Christ's words always have on those who love Him.

Take some time to examine your spiritual life. Are you too busy "serving" Christ to know Christ as you should? Perhaps it's time to *enjoy* Him for a while.

LUKE 10:40

Martha was distracted with much serving, and she approached Him and said, "Lord, do You not care that my sister has left me to serve alone? Therefore tell her to help me."

M artha's external behavior at first appeared to be true servanthood. She was the one who put on the apron and went to work in the task of serving others. But her treatment of Mary soon revealed a serious defect in her servant's heart. She allowed herself to become censorious and sharp-tongued. Such words in front of other guests were certain to humiliate Mary. She was also wrong in her judgment of Mary, assuming her to be lazy, when in fact Mary was the one whose heart was in the right place.

Martha's rebuke shows how subtly and sinfully human pride can corrupt even the best of our actions. In a very practical sense, Martha was acting as a servant to all, but the focus of her heart and attention shifted from Christ to herself, and she reverted to anger, resentment, jealousy, distrust, a critical spirit, judgmentalism, and unkindness—all in a matter of minutes.

JOHN 12:7–8

Jesus said, "Let her alone; she has kept this [perfume] for the day of My burial. For the poor you have with you always, but Me you do not have always."

M ary, in contrast to Martha, was so consumed with thoughts of Christ that she became completely oblivious to everything else. She sat at His feet and listened to Him intently, absorbing His every word and nuance. She was by no means being lazy. She simply understood the true importance of this occasion. The Son of God Himself was a guest in her home. Listening to Him and worshiping Him were at the moment the very best use of Mary's energies and the one right place for her to focus her attention.

Notice that Jesus didn't rebuke Martha's choice to serve, only her prideful decision to rebuke Mary. Neither did He suggest that serving Him and the other houseguests was a poor use of her time. After all, someone had to get things done. However, He did take the opportunity to establish priorities. Worship must come first, then serving. Perhaps if Martha had spent some time at Jesus' feet, pride would not have tainted her service so quickly.

PSALM 95:6–7

Oh come, let us worship and bow down;
Let us kneel before the LORD our Maker.
For He is our God,
And we are the people of His pasture,
And the sheep of His hand.

M artha's feelings were natural and somewhat understandable. I suspect that many women would be inclined to sympathize with Martha, not Mary. After all, it would normally be considered rude to let your sister do all the hard work in the kitchen while you sit chatting with guests. Nevertheless, what Mary was doing was better still.

It is a danger, even for people who love Christ, that we not become so concerned with doing things for Him that we begin to neglect hearing Him and remembering what He has done for us. We must never allow our service for Christ to crowd out our worship of Him. The moment our works become more important to us than our worship, we have turned the true spiritual priorities on their heads.

EPHESIANS 2:8–9

For by grace you have been saved through faith, and that not of yourselves; it is the gift of God, not of works, lest anyone should boast.

Martha's "much serving" was a distraction from the "one thing" that was really needed—listening to and learning from Jesus. Religious works often have a sinister tendency to eclipse faith itself. Proper good works always flow from faith and are the fruit of it. But faith must come first and is the only viable foundation for true and lasting good works.

Human instinct seems to tell us that what we *do* is more important than what we *believe*. But the reverse is true. Martha seems to have forgotten these things momentarily. She was acting as if Christ needed her to work for Him more than she needed His work on her behalf. Rather than humbly fixing her faith on the vital importance of Christ's work for sinners, she was thinking too much in terms of what she could do for Him. Unfortunately, this tendency is alive and all too active today.

PROVERBS 14:11–12

The house of the wicked will be overthrown,
But the tent of the upright will flourish.
There is a way that seems right to a man,
But its end is the way of death.

Simon the Zealot was apparently a one-time member of the political party known as the Zealots. The historian Josephus described the Zealots as more politically minded than any other group except their opposites, the Herodians. They hated the Romans, and their goal was to overthrow Roman occupation. They advanced their agenda primarily through terrorism and covert acts of violence.

The Zealots' desire for Israel was good. They wanted to eliminate foreign rule in order to reestablish Israel's theocracy, with God as King. That is what they expected the Messiah to do—and what He *will* do at His second advent. However, their methods had not been commanded by God. They presumed to accomplish God's objective through their own methods by their own power. And that's always a recipe for unimaginable evil.

ROMANS 12:17–18

Repay no one evil for evil. Have regard for good things in the sight of all men. If it is possible, as much as depends on you, live peaceably with all men.

The Zealots believed that only God Himself had the right to rule over Jews and that paying tribute to a pagan king was an act of treason against God. They carried out guerilla-style warfare and terrorist attacks to achieve independence, believing they were doing God's work by assassinating Roman soldiers, political leaders, and anyone else who opposed them. The Zealots were expecting a Messiah who would lead them in overthrowing the Romans and then restoring the kingdom of Israel.

While these men were passionate, courageous, and completely dedicated to accomplishing a worthy goal, they were nonetheless *wrong*! They operated outside God's plan, and their failure only intensified the Roman occupation.

Christians are called to be ambassadors of "peace with God" (Romans 5:1). We're not commissioned by Christ to be political activists, insurrectionists, or rebels against the powers that be. If we bear that in mind, we'll avoid the error of the Zealots.

PROVERBS 28:13–14

He who covers his sins will not prosper,
But whoever confesses and forsakes them will have mercy.
Happy is the man who is always reverent,
But he who hardens his heart will fall into calamity.

It is interesting that when Matthew and Mark list the Twelve, they list Simon the Zealot just before Judas Iscariot. They probably both originally followed Christ for similar political reasons. When Jesus did not overthrow Rome, but instead talked of dying, some might have expected Simon to betray Him, but that was *before* he met Jesus. Somewhere along the line, Simon became a genuine believer and was transformed. Judas Iscariot never really believed.

Two people can come from similar backgrounds and influences yet have completely different reactions to their encounters with Christ. One may believe and become radically transformed. Another will be hardened, allowing his sin to set like concrete, impenetrable to grace and cold to God's touch. The difference would seem to be how each person regards sin. Simon saw his sin as deadly and then fled to find refuge in His Savior.

What place does sin have in your life? Secret friend or mortal enemy?

ISAIAH 11:1, 6

There shall come forth a Rod from the stem of Jesse,
And a Branch shall grow out of his roots. . . .
"The wolf also shall dwell with the lamb,
The leopard shall lie down with the young goat,
The calf and the young lion and the fatling together;
And a little child shall lead them."

Of course, as one of the Twelve, Simon also had to associate with Matthew, who was at the opposite end of the political spectrum, collecting taxes for the Roman government. At one point in his life, Simon would probably have gladly killed Matthew. In the end, they became spiritual brethren, working side by side for the same cause—the spread of the gospel—and worshiping the same Lord.

The bond shared by the Twelve was a model of the church they would help start, and the church is a foretaste of the kingdom. Individually, the lives of kingdom citizens are a wonderful testimony to the saving grace of God and the inevitable triumph of His kingdom. Collectively, the power of that testimony is exponentially greater.

MARK 16:15–16

And [Jesus] said to [His disciples], "Go into all the world and preach the gospel to every creature. He who believes and is baptized will be saved; but he who does not believe will be condemned."

It was amazing that Jesus would select a man like Simon to be an apostle. But he was a man of fierce loyalties, amazing passion, courage, and zeal. Simon had believed the truth and embraced Christ as his Lord. The fiery enthusiasm he once had for Israel was now expressed in his devotion to Christ.

Several sources say that after the destruction of Jerusalem, Simon took the gospel north and preached in the British Isles. Like so many others, Simon disappears from the biblical record. There is no reliable record of what happened to him, but all accounts say he was killed for preaching the gospel. This man who was once willing to kill and be killed for a political agenda within the confines of Judea found a more fruitful cause for which to give his life—in the proclamation of salvation for sinners out of every nation, tongue, and tribe.

PROVERBS 22:1

A good name is to be chosen rather than great riches,
Loving favor rather than silver and gold.

The last name on the list of faithful disciples is "Judas, the son of James." The name *Judas* in and of itself is a fine name. It means "Yahweh leads." But because of the treachery of Judas Iscariot, the name *Judas* will forever bear a negative connotation.

Judas the son of James actually had three names. Matthew calls him "Lebbaeus, whose surname was Thaddaeus," but Judas was likely his given name. *Thaddaeus* means "breast child"—evoking the idea of a nursing baby. It almost has a derisive sound, like "mama's boy." His other name, *Lebbaeus*, is similar. It is from a Hebrew root that refers to the heart—literally, "heart child." Both names suggest he had a tender, childlike heart.

When people utter your name—both now and when you have departed this life—what image do you hope they will recall? What are you doing to give them the memories you would most like them to have after you are gone?

ROMANS 12:4-5

*For as we have many members in one body, but all the members do not have
the same function, so we, being many, are one body in Christ, and
individually members of one another.*

I t is interesting to think of such a gentle soul as Lebbaeus
Thaddaeus hanging around in the same group of apostles as
Simon the Zealot. Zealots make great preachers. But so do tenderhearted, compassionate, gentle, sweet-spirited souls like "Judas the
son of James." Together they contribute to a very complex and
intriguing group of twelve apostles. There's at least one of every
imaginable personality. Yet they all had one thing in common: they
had forsaken the world to follow Christ.

It is just like the Lord to bring opposites together to accomplish
His purposes—so unlike our way, which is to mistake uniformity
for compatibility. The Lord—infinitely creative in His fashioning
of people and molding their personalities—delights to form these
vibrant teams, whose ability to form a unit and accomplish great
things is fueled by their differences.

JOHN 14:21

[Jesus said,] "He who has My commandments and keeps them, it is he who loves Me. And he who loves Me will be loved by My Father, and I will love him and manifest Myself to him."

On the eve of Jesus' trial and subsequent crucifixion, He gathered the Twelve for a last evening of instruction and encouragement, although few if any understood the significance of the Last Supper. When Jesus announced His going away, Lebbaeus Thaddaeus responded with tenderhearted humility. "Lord, how is it that You will manifest Yourself to us, and not to the world?"

Judas the son of James couldn't believe that Jesus would manifest Himself to this ragtag group of eleven and not to the whole world. Of course, the gentle disciple didn't take into account Jesus' resurrection, the coming of the Holy Spirit, the establishment of the church, and the Lord's dramatic reappearance at the Second Coming. He, like the other disciples, had a different plan in mind.

The same can be true of our own lives. We have a vision of how life will play out that's good yet incongruent with how God wants events to unfold. The question is, are we going to get on His program or fight for our own?

JOHN 14:22

Judas (not Iscariot) said to Him, "Lord, how is it that You will manifest Yourself to us, and not to the world?"

A t Jesus' last meal with His disciples, He announced His going away, which left them perplexed. And here we see the tenderhearted humility of Labbaeus Thaddaeus. He doesn't say anything brash or bold or overconfident like the others. He doesn't rebuke the Lord like Peter once did. His question is full of gentleness and meekness and devoid of any sort of pride. He asked the question that weighed heavily on his heart. After all, Jesus was the Savior of the world, the rightful heir of the earth, the King of kings. Thaddaeus held great hope for the world; but Jesus' announcement left him confused. This was a pious, believing disciple with an honest question. And Jesus' answer was as tender as the question.

Sometimes we too find ourselves dazed and confused by events, left wondering, *What's happening, Lord? This is not what I expected.* God's heart is warmed by such honest, childlike submission and trust. He welcomes the opportunity to teach a pliable heart—including yours.

JOHN 14:23

Jesus answered and said to him, "If anyone loves Me, he will keep My word; and My Father will love him, and We will come to him and make Our home with him."

When Labbaeus Thaddaeus asked his honest, tender-hearted question, Jesus gave him a marvelous answer. Christ would indeed reveal Himself to the whole world. He will manifest Himself to anyone who loves Him.

Judas the son of James was still thinking in the political and material realm. "How come You haven't taken over the world yet? Why don't You just manifest Yourself to the world?" Jesus' answer meant, "I'm not going to take over the world externally; I'm going to take over hearts, one at a time." Then He linked love to obedience to discipleship and announced the coming of the Holy Spirit to dwell within every heart submitted to the Father and the Son. While the disciples hoped for a political and military solution to the world's problems, God had a more perfect solution. (He always does!) He would conquer the hearts of people and transform them to obey willingly.

Hopefully, He has conquered yours already.

JOHN 14:26–27

*[Jesus said to His disciples,] "The Helper, the Holy Spirit, whom the
Father will send in My name, He will teach you all things, and bring to
your remembrance all things that I said to you. Peace I leave with you, My
peace I give to you; not as the world gives do I give to you. Let not your
heart be troubled, neither let it be afraid."*

M ost of the early tradition about Lebbaeus Thaddaeus suggests that a few years after Pentecost, he took the gospel
north to Edessa, a royal city in Mesopotamia, in the region of
Turkey today. There are numerous ancient accounts of how he
healed the king of Edessa, a man named Abgar. In the fourth century, Eusebius the historian said the archives at Edessa (now
destroyed) contained full records of Thaddaeus's visit and the healing of Abgar. The traditional apostolic symbol of Judas Lebbaeus
Thaddaeus is a club, because tradition says he was clubbed to death
for his faith.

Thus this tenderhearted soul followed his Lord faithfully to
the end. His testimony was as powerful and far-reaching as that
of the better-known and more outspoken disciples. He, like
them, is proof of how God uses perfectly ordinary people in
remarkable ways.

ACTS 16:14

Now a certain woman named Lydia heard us. She was a seller of purple
from the city of Thyatira, who worshiped God. The Lord opened her heart
to heed the things spoken by Paul.

Lydia is best remembered as the original convert for the gospel in Europe. She was the first person on record to respond to the message of Christ during the apostle Paul's original missionary journey into Europe. Ironically, however, Lydia herself was not European. Her hometown was the city of Thyatira in the region of Asia Minor. Instead of reaching Lydia in the region she regarded as home, the gospel pursued her to Europe, where she was engaged in business.

Lydia was a remarkable woman who appears suddenly and unexpectedly in the biblical narrative, reminding us that while God's sovereign purposes usually remain hidden from our eyes, He is always at work in the secret and surprising ways to call out a people for His name. This was true of Lydia, and it is true of you as well. To redeem you, He first sought you, using all circumstances to bring you to Himself.

ACTS 16:9–10

A vision appeared to Paul in the night. A man of Macedonia stood and pleaded with him, saying, "Come over to Macedonia and help us." Now after he had seen the vision, immediately we sought to go to Macedonia, concluding that the Lord had called us to preach the gospel to them.

The sovereign hand of God's providential guidance was evident to Paul's entire group. Luke didn't explain all the circumstances, but by some means they had been forbidden by the Spirit of God to journey into the heart of Asia Minor. That's when Paul received a revelation calling him across to the European continent. God had made it perfectly clear to all that there was just one way ahead—Macedonia (present-day Greece).

From a human standpoint, Asia Minor was the more logical place to go next. Covering the territory between Jerusalem and Rome, working east to west, would allow Paul's entourage to spend more time evangelizing and less time traveling. But the Lord's plan was better. Paul would reach Asia Minor in due time, but there were people in the western empire who were ready to hear the gospel—Lydia being the first.

JOHN 15:16

You did not choose Me, but I chose you and appointed you that you should go and bear fruit, and that your fruit should remain, that whatever you ask the Father in My name He may give you.

P aul met Lydia in Philippi when he sought out the place where Jewish women from the area gathered to pray. She was a Gentile worshiper of YHWH but had not yet committed to become a Jewish proselyte. This influence apparently prepared her to hear the good news concerning the Messiah. Luke recorded that Lydia "heard us" using a Greek word that meant she was listening intently. She didn't merely absorb the sound, but she was carefully attentive to the meaning of the words.

The manner of Lydia's conversion is a fine illustration of how God always redeems lost souls. From our human perspective, we may think we are seeking Him, that trusting Christ is a merely a "decision" that lies within the power of our own will to choose, or that we are sovereign over our own hearts and affections. In reality, whenever you see a soul like Lydia's truly seeking God, you can be certain God is drawing her.

ACTS 16:15

When she and her household were baptized, she begged us, saying, "If you have judged me to be faithful to the Lord, come to my house and stay." So she persuaded us.

L ydia's faith was immediately evident in her actions. Almost incidentally, Luke stated that her entire household followed her in baptism, which reveals a great deal. Lydia appears to have been a widow, so her household may have been home to children but certainly included servants. She was already leading others to Christ. Furthermore, she was quick to show hospitality to the missionaries, prevailing upon them to stay in her home.

Paul and the missionaries apparently stayed with Lydia for a long time, and her home became their base of operations for the region. Lydia's wonderful act of hospitality opened the way for the church to penetrate Europe. Thus, even if Lydia had never spoken of Christ to another person, she nonetheless won countless thousands to the Lord by her faithful support of God's full-time missionaries.

So [Paul and Silas] went out of the prison and entered the house of Lydia;
and when they had seen the brethren, they encouraged them and departed.

The evangelism of Paul and Silas eventually landed them in the Philippian jail. After they were supernaturally released and then brought the jailer to faith in Christ, the two men quickly made their way back to Lydia's house. Apparently, her home was the customary meeting place of the church in that area, so that is where Paul and Silas met with the body of believers before departing.

The real cost of Lydia's discipleship and hospitality was potentially much higher than the monetary value of room and board for a group of missionaries. If preaching the gospel was deemed a jailable offense, Lydia was exposing herself to possible trouble—a loss of business, bad will in the community, and even a prison sentence for herself—by housing these strangers and thus giving them a base from which to evangelize.

I have no doubt a smart businesswoman like Lydia was well aware of the risk and had counted the potential cost. Still, discipleship was her chosen path, no matter what the cost.

LUKE 1:48–49

For [God] has regarded the lowly state of His maidservant;
For behold, henceforth all generations will call me blessed.
For He who is mighty has done great things for me,
And holy is His name.

Of all the extraordinary women in Scripture, one stands out above all others as the most blessed, most highly favored by God. Indeed, no woman is more truly remarkable than Mary. She was the one sovereignly chosen by God—from among all the women who have ever been born—to be the instrument through which He would bring the Messiah into the world. Mary testified that all generations would regard her as profoundly blessed by God, not because she was a saintly superhuman, but because she was given such remarkable grace and privilege.

The very nature of grace is blessing without any merit on the part of the receiver, yet many Christians behave as though they deserve the goodness God has bestowed upon them. Furthermore, they resent the loss of good things, which they feel entitled to receive! Mary's humility is an example to all of us. If anyone could presume to boast, it is no one more than the mother of Christ.

LUKE 1:38

Mary said, "Behold the maidservant of the Lord! Let it be to me according to your word." And the angel departed from her.

Mary is the equivalent of the Hebrew "Miriam." The name may be derived from the Hebrew word for "bitter." Her young life may well have been filled with bitter hardships. Her hometown was a forlorn community in a poor district of Galilee. Nazareth famously bore the brunt of one disciple's disdain, which was apparently a common opinion of the tiny town.

Mary's life was like everything else connected with the birth of Christ: humble, obscure, unpretentious, and unexpected. Mary herself, on the other hand, could not have been a more fitting means of bringing the Savior into the world. She was a virgin, she was a woman of uncommon devotion to God, and she was willing to serve the Lord without reservation or condition.

May all of us be willing to say with Mary, "Let it be to me according to Your Word, Lord."

MATTHEW 1:18

Now the birth of Jesus Christ was as follows: After His mother Mary was betrothed to Joseph, before they came together, she was found with child of the Holy Spirit.

During the betrothal period—usually a year—the couple lived in their respective households but were considered husband and wife by law. During this time, they were not to have sexual relations at all. In fact, one of the main points of the betrothal period was to demonstrate the fidelity of both partners.

Common sense suggests that Mary must have anticipated the inevitable cultural and social difficulties she would face the moment the angel told her that she would conceive a child. Her joy and amazement at learning that she would be the mother of the Redeemer might therefore have been crushed by the horror of the scandal that awaited her. Still, nothing could compare with the immense privilege of becoming the mother of the Christ.

This would be the first example of how receiving the King of heaven would put an individual at odds with an unbelieving world. And it certainly wasn't going to be the last.

MATTHEW 1:19–20

Then Joseph her husband, being a just man, and not wanting to make her a public example, was minded to put her away secretly. But while he thought about these things, behold, an angel of the Lord appeared to him in a dream, saying, "Joseph, son of David, do not be afraid to take to you Mary your wife, for that which is conceived in her is of the Holy Spirit."

Mary was betrothed to Joseph, about whom we know next to nothing—except that he was a carpenter and a righteous man. Scripture is very clear in teaching that Mary was still a virgin when Jesus was miraculously conceived in her womb. The Greek term allows for no subtle nuance of meaning, and her own testimony is that she had never been physically intimate with a man. Both were godly Jews from respectable families. Ironically, their wonderful, miraculous blessing would be perceived as sin by others.

Sometimes the truth we hold will be doubted or denied by others—perhaps even by those we love most. When we have exhausted all reasonable attempts to share the truth with others, we must then stand firmly on what we know, accept that misunderstanding is a difficult yet normal part of life. Then, the truth we hold becomes an opportunity for greater intimacy with the Author of truth, our Savior.

ROMANS 8:18

I consider that the sufferings of this present time are not worthy to be compared with the glory which shall be revealed in us.

There's no evidence that Mary ever brooded over the effects her pregnancy would have on her reputation. She instantly, humbly, and joyfully submitted to God's will without further doubt or question. She could hardly have had a more godly response to the announcement of Jesus' birth. It demonstrated that she was a young woman of mature faith and one who was a worshiper of the true God. Her great joy over the Lord's plan for her would soon be very evident.

Great spiritual blessing often places a strain on our relationship with the world, which chooses to reject Christ and all that He calls us to honor. Nevertheless, the joy of knowing Him overwhelmingly outweighs the difficulties imposed on us by a world that hates Him. Remember that, and be faithful.

LUKE 1:46–48

Mary said: "My soul magnifies the Lord, and my spirit has rejoiced in God my Savior. For He has regarded the lowly state of His maidservant; for behold, henceforth all generations will call me blessed."

It is clear that Mary's young heart and mind were already thoroughly saturated with the Word of God. In her "Magnificat," she included not only echoes of two of Hannah's prayers (1 Samuel 1:11; 2:1–10), but also several other allusions to the Law, the Psalms, and the Prophets. It was customary in Jewish prayers to recite God's past faithfulness to His people. Mary followed that convention by recalling how God had helped Israel and praising the fulfillment of His promises.

Mary's response is such an admirable example for us. Whether in sorrow or joy, Scripture poured out of her as naturally as tears or laughter. The first words on her lips are the Word of God, not because she was morally superior, but because she had diligently filled her heart with the Law, the Psalms, and the Prophets.

LUKE 2:48–49

So when [Mary and Joseph] saw Him, they were amazed; and His mother said to Him, "Son, why have You done this to us? Look, Your father and I have sought You anxiously." And He said to them, "Why did you seek Me? Did you not know that I must be about My Father's business?"

Throughout Jesus' ministry, Mary struggled to understand her place in her Son's life. As a man, He was her Son. As God, He was her Lord. Her dilemma was one no other parent can fully appreciate. On three separate occasions, He gently and respectfully reminded her of His identity and mission on earth (Luke 2:41–49; John 2:1–12; Mark 3:31–35). Eventually, she became one of His faithful disciples and came to grips with the reality that He had work to do.

Just like Mary, we often fail to recognize our place in the Lord's life. (We usually have that backwards!) This leads to a spirit of entitlement in which we presume to give God instructions in our prayers rather than ask for wisdom to know His will. Mary's life is an illustration of spiritual growth, whereby we recognize Jesus as Lord and submit to His authority.

LUKE 2:34–35

Then Simeon blessed them, and said to Mary His mother, "Behold, this Child is destined for the fall and rising of many in Israel, and for a sign which will be spoken against (yes, a sword will pierce through your own soul also), that the thoughts of many hearts may be revealed."

Undoubtedly, Mary had an inkling that this day would come. When Jesus was yet a newborn infant, His Spirit of God had revealed to Simeon that he would have the privilege of seeing the Messiah before he died. When he saw the infant Jesus, Simeon uttered a prophecy that undoubtedly remained in Mary's mind through the years.

At the end of Jesus' earthly ministry, Mary stood watching as a soldier thrust a sword into Jesus' side. She must have truly felt as if a sword had pierced her own soul also. At that very moment, she might well have recalled Simeon's prophecy, and suddenly its true meaning came home to her with full force. Her Son, the Christ, had come to die for the sins of the world, including her own.

JOHN 19:26–27

When Jesus therefore saw His mother, and the disciple whom He loved standing by, He said to His mother, "Woman, behold your son!" Then He said to the disciple, "Behold your mother!" And from that hour that disciple took her to his own home.

Mary seemed to understand that her steadfast presence at Jesus' side was the only kind of support she could give Him at this dreaded moment. But even that was merely a public show of *support*. Mary's personal suffering did not represent any kind of participation in His atoning work. He was bearing the sins of the world. As a matter of fact, in the waning hours of Jesus' life, He spotted Mary standing nearby with a small group of women and John, the beloved disciple. For the final time, Jesus acknowledged His human relationship with Mary. So one of Jesus' last earthly acts before yielding up His life to God was to make sure that for the rest of her life, Mary would be cared for.

The act epitomizes Mary's relationship with her firstborn Son. She was His earthly mother; but He was her eternal Lord.

LUKE 1:38

Mary said [to the angel], "Behold the maidservant of the Lord! Let it be to me according to your word."

Mary was like no other mother. Godly mothers are typically absorbed in the task of training their children for heaven. Mary's Son was the Lord and Creator of heaven. Over time she came to perceive the full import of that truth until it filled her heart. She became a disciple and a worshiper. Her maternal relationship with Him faded into the background. That moment on the cross—Jesus placing His mother into the earthly care of John—formally marked the end of that earthly aspect of Mary's relationship with Jesus.

Mary herself never claimed to be, or pretended to be, anything more than a humble handmaiden of the Lord. She was extraordinary because God used her in an extraordinary way. The lowly perspective reflected in Mary's Magnificat is the same simple spirit of humility that colored all her life and character. And anyone who is blessed to be an instrument of grace in God's hands would do well to emulate her.

JAMES 5:17–18

Elijah was a man with a nature like ours, and he prayed earnestly that it would not rain; and it did not rain on the land for three years and six months. And he prayed again, and the heaven gave rain, and the earth produced its fruit.

In the gospel accounts, the disciples were usually in the background of the narrative. When they do come to the foreground, it is often to manifest doubt, disbelief, or confusion. Sometimes we see them thinking more highly of themselves than they ought to think. Sometimes they speak when they ought to remain silent and seem clueless about things they ought to have understood. Sometimes they exhibit more confidence in their own abilities and their own strengths than they should. So their shortcomings and weaknesses show up more often than their strengths. In that sense, the raw honesty of the gospel accounts is amazing.

Frankly, I'm encouraged by this. They are a lot like us! I love that the Bible doesn't flatter its heroes. The men and women described in the pages of Scripture were not superhuman; however, they did become remarkable examples of how trusting God can accomplish supernatural results.

[The Christians in Jerusalem] continued steadfastly in the apostles' doctrine and fellowship, in the breaking of bread, and in prayers. Then fear came upon every soul, and many wonders and signs were done through the apostles.

There are very few manifestations of any great acts by the apostles. We are told that they were empowered to heal, raise the dead, and cast out demons, but even that is narrated in such a way as to highlight the apostle's imperfections (cf. Mark 9:14–29). The one place in all the Gospels where a specific apostle does something truly extraordinary is when Peter began to walk on the water—but he immediately found himself sinking.

The gospel records simply do not portray these men as heroes. Their heroism played out after Jesus went back to heaven, sent the Holy Spirit, and empowered them. Suddenly we begin to see them acting differently. They are strong and courageous. They perform great miracles. They preach with a newfound boldness.

Such a dramatic change invites the question: What happened? Put simply, the day of Pentecost. The Holy Spirit arrived with power and, oh, the difference He makes! If only we would yield to Him, how different would be our homes, our churches, our world?

2 CORINTHIANS 4:7

We have this treasure in earthen vessels, that the excellence of the power may be of God and not of us.

It must be borne in mind that the apostles were men who gave up everything to follow Christ. Peter spoke for them all when he said, "See, we have left all and followed You" (Luke 18:28). They had left houses, jobs, lands, family, and friends to follow Christ. Their sacrifice was heroic. With the exception of Judas Iscariot, they all became valiant and intrepid witnesses.

We don't actually see much of their heroism in the gospel records, because the gospel writers honestly portrayed their weaknesses as well as their strengths. The apostles are not presented to us as mythic figures, but as real people. They are not depicted as prominent celebrities, but as ordinary men. That is why, as far as the gospel accounts are concerned, the apostles give color and life to the descriptions of Jesus' life, because they are like us. The implied message, then, is this: you can become like them, ordinary people whom Christ has made extraordinary.